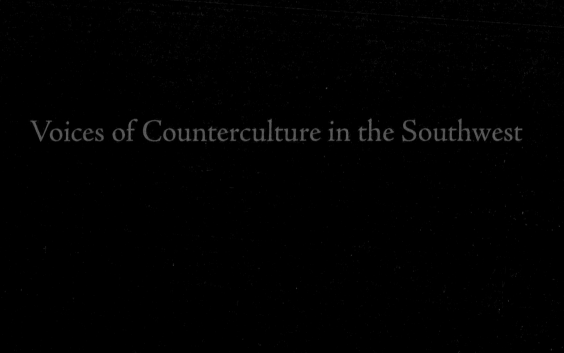

Voices of Counterculture in the Southwest

Voices of Counterculture in the Southwest

EDITED BY JACK LOEFFLER AND
MEREDITH DAVIDSON

Museum of New Mexico Press
Santa Fe

CONTENTS

ACKNOWLEDGMENTS

WE ARE GRATEFUL to all of the essayists who contributed their invaluable perspectives to this book: Yvonne Bond, Peter Coyote, Lisa Law, Peter Rowan, Siddiq Hans von Briesen, Art Kopecky, Bill Steen, Sylvia Rodríguez, Enrique Lamadrid, Levi Romero, the late Rina Swentzell, and Gary Paul Nabhan. We also wish to express our thanks to all the participants whose interviews we have excerpted: Rick Klein, the late Philip Whalen, Gary Snyder, Shonto Begay, Camillus Lopez, Tara Evonne Trudell, the late Roberta Blackgoat, Richard Grow, Alvin Josephy, David Brower, Edward Abbey, Dave Foreman, Elinor Ostrom, Fritjof Capra, and Melissa Savage. We thank the photographers for their invaluable contributions: Lisa Law, Seth Roffman, Terrence Moore, Cesar Estrada, Tom Alexander, and the late Karl Kernberger.

We are grateful to Lisa Pacheco and Anna Gallegos at the Museum of New Mexico Press for seeing this project through to fruition. And *mil gracias* to David Skolkin for his superb design of this book.

We express our heartfelt thanks to Beth Hadas, editor *extraordinaire* for her relentless commitment to clarity.

We are grateful to Andrew Wulf, director of the New Mexico History Museum, for his support of the counterculture project.

And we wish to express our deep gratitude to the Museum of New Mexico Foundation and The Christensen Fund of San Francisco for providing the necessary funding to make this book possible.

Thank you one and all!

It was a High Time in Northern New Mexico

MEREDITH DAVIDSON

> *It was a high time in northern New Mexico.*
> —JIM LEVY, 2009

On Sunday, April 26, 1970 . . . we were accosted by four drunk young men between the ages of 19 and 24. I was asked if I intended to get my hair cut or were they going to cut it for me. . . . Before I had a chance to answer I received a fist in the nose. Two of the men came in my side of the truck forcing open the door. . . . As if by signal a red Mustang drove up driven by a fifth man and the four (attackers) jumped in and sped off. Of course the cause is obvious. Prejudice and hatred. It is not the people who hit us who are to blame but everything which has produced this terrible situation. Given what is going on in the world this is not an isolated act, but part of a much larger pattern.

> —STEPHEN DURKEE, 1970

EXCERPTED FROM THE SMALL UNDERGROUND Taos newspaper *Fountain of Light*, Durkee's story illustrates the underbelly of the counterculture movement of the time. The reactions to those who rejected mainstream culture went beyond playful cartoons about patchouli oil or harmless satire about drifters. There was real violence and conflict. During the 1960s and '70s, countless young people, resisting the 1950s values of their parents, turned to alternative ways of living, standing up against the ongoing war and voicing their views through public demonstrations for civil and social rights. Tension and violence resulted, nationally and locally in New Mexico. Stories like Durkee's help dispel the myth of tricultural harmony promoted in tourist literature about the Southwest. The exhibit at the New Mexico History Museum and the Palace of the Governors (2017) and the work you are about to read bring to light the personal experiences of the individuals who lived through this era: a not-so-distant past that continues to influence us today.

In 2011, I worked on the twentieth floor of a New York City building, furiously transcribing oral histories at the National September 11 Memorial and Museum. After spending hours pulling out memories of favorite pastimes, holidays, and traditions recounted by people who had lost family members in the 2001 attacks, I would leave my office late and pass crowds of people in front of my building across Zuccotti Park. Men and women, my age and younger, were there as part of Occupy Wall Street, which I saw as a somewhat disorganized movement calling attention to the dysfunction of our economic system. Over the autumn and early winter there were several clashes between the protesters and the New York City police. On December 31, 2011, nearly five hundred protesters attempted to reoccupy the park, having been evicted earlier that month. More than sixty Occupiers were arrested, and when I returned to work in the New Year, the park was once again home to pigeons rather than protesters.

At the time, I didn't get it. I didn't understand what the protesters were hoping to accomplish, and I would have put myself in the "Get a job" category of commentators. There was something about listening to the voices of families affected by the attacks that inhibited my ability to see the direct connection to what was happening below. The protesters were challenging the economic systems that had in some ways made us a target in the first place—a logical connection I just wasn't making.

How does that connection apply to the essays and voices in this collection? Well, we are the products of our past, but we are also shaped by the stories we choose to engage with and explore. Seeking the individual within the context of the times is what interested me as we began to explore the countercultural narrative here in the Southwest. I am drawn to the voices of those who passed through Lama, New Buffalo, and other communal stomping grounds and the voices of those who sought knowledge from La Academia de la Nueva Raza (the Academy of the New Humanity). We can learn from these accounts not just the historic happenings, but the flavor of the era and the feel of the urge to create cultural change. Each story adds to the prism of the 1960s and '70s in the nation and across the Southwest. The authors speak about personal relationships and connections. They explore what led individuals to migrate from the coasts to the Southwest or through Mexico and back. All carry the thread of wanting to fit in by the very act of resisting *something*.

Peter Coyote notes in his contribution the distinct challenge of contributing a fresh view on the idea of counterculture or the 1960s. But I argue that we are in a moment of relevance in this decade of the twenty-first century. Fifty years after the Summer of Love, the youth of today's world are facing similar issues of racial prejudice, global violence, and environmental challenges. Blogs and websites explore tiny-house living and homesteading. It seems we are once again seeking a more wholesome approach to living and an awareness of something greater than ourselves.

The stereotype of a Me Generation is undermined by the gathering of anti–Wall Street advocates and groups standing up against systematic violence against our own citizens. We may be more likely to see an opinion in a hashtag or an online rant than in an underground paper, but it is my hope that by examining the roots of these passions in the counterculture of the past, we can better understand how to move forward today.

Recently I read a piece about former hippies carrying on the work of their youth in what Buddhists might call Right Livelihood. The Buddha encouraged his disciples to make their living in a way that would not cause harm and ideally that could prove to be ethically positive. We see this work in the continuation of each contributor's path in these essays. Perhaps by engaging with the stories here, we can understand the roots of this idealism that for a full generation influenced droves of young people seeking something better.

Let me conclude with another excerpt from the same short-lived Taos newspaper: "Our concern is with the real—real food grown by ourselves for the most part, real and useful products produced by heads and hands and hearts, expressions in art forms that manifest individual energies of human beings rather than the faceless and soulless work of mechanized existence. To plant and cultivate and to ultimately harvest worthwhile things from joyous labors, this is what we are about" ("Why Taos?," *Fountain of Light*, 1969).

PART I. PERSONAL REFLECTIONS

1

Headed into the Wind

JACK LOEFFLER

I WAS A SEVENTEEN-YEAR-OLD SENIOR in high school when I received news that I had failed my aptitude test. The test had revealed that my career preference was bifurcated between being a jazz trumpet player and a forest ranger. According to those who were purported to know better, I was assailed by conflicting absolutes. One cannot *want* to be both a jazz trumpet player *and* a forest ranger. It was that notification of failure that began to confirm what I had long suspected—I didn't fit in. My aspirations didn't coincide with cultural expectations. This was in 1954 in Manchester, Connecticut, where my family had moved from Columbus, Ohio, immediately following the end of World War II.

It took two more years before I decided to drop out of college, volunteer for the draft (every American male was conscripted to serve in the armed forces), and spend the next two years as a trumpet-playing army bandsman. After sixteen weeks of basic training at Fort Benning, Georgia, I was shipped out to Fort Lewis, Washington, where I became a member of the 21st Army Band. A few days thereafter, alone in the barracks, I was running some jazz riffs through my horn. A black sergeant sat down on a nearby cot and listened for a while.

"Hey, man. You wanna join my group?" he asked after a few minutes.

I knew that he was the lead clarinet player in the military band, that he was known as Steve, and that he outranked me by five grades. I didn't know that he was also a fine jazz alto sax player.

"Well, thanks. What kind of group is it, Sarge?"

"Cool it on the 'Sarge' bullshit, man. My name's Steve, and we play jazz."

"Yeah. I'd really like to join your group."

And I began to play real jazz with a quintet of fellow jazz musicians who were all in the army. My jazz trumpet hero was then—and remains—Clifford Brown, a jazz genius who had died in a car wreck on the Pennsylvania Turnpike less than a year earlier, when he was only twenty-five years old. He has now inspired three generations of jazz trumpet players.

Then it was over. The 21st Army Band was suddenly disbanded, and we were all sent to different points on the military horizon. I never saw Steve again, but I remain grateful for his fine jazz tutelage to this day.

In July 1957, I was sent to Camp Irwin, in the Mojave Desert about thirty-seven miles from Barstow, California. I had just turned twenty-one and been promoted to private first class. I checked into band headquarters, was assigned a bed in the air-conditioned barracks, was issued short sleeve shirts, Bermuda shorts, and a pith helmet, and thus became a desert rat, which I remain to this day.

My first gig with the 433rd Army Band was to travel by bus to a place called Desert Rock at the Nevada Proving Grounds, not too far from Las Vegas. The following morning before dawn, our band was assembled, and we began to perform Sousa marches from memory. Suddenly the sky lit up brighter than the sun, and we all watched as a great mushroom cloud unfurled skyward displaying an array of colors I cannot describe. As I watched the aboveground detonation of an atomic bomb a scant seven miles away, I had my great and enduring epiphany. I came to realize that I was sane in a culture gone deeply awry. The atomic bomb, designed to kill many thousands of fellow humans in a single blast, also took out every iota of life in the immediate habitat and rendered the habitat itself unlivable for many years. And thus I became and remain what we now call a counterculturalist, though the term was only coined a dozen years later by Theodore Roszak.

I got out of the army in 1958 and went first to Santa Barbara and then to North Beach in San Francisco. I had a little bread in my pocket from my army discharge pay. I had my horn, and I had a short—a 1952 Pontiac sedan that I could sleep in. I found a place called the Coffee Gallery where I could jam with fellow jazz musicians. I could eat my one big meal a day—a five-course Italian dinner with a half-carafe of wine at the Green Mountain Restaurant for a buck and a quarter. I could listen to poetry being read in any of a number of coffeehouses and hangouts, including both the Caffe Trieste and the Co-Existence Bagel Shop. And I could browse endlessly in the City Lights Bookstore, owned by Lawrence Ferlinghetti.

While still in the army, I read "Howl," by Allen Ginsberg, and was blown away by his condemnation of contemporary society. In North Beach, I listened to a poet named Philip Whalen read from his own work. Philip was one of the five poets (the others were Gary Snyder, Philip Lamantia, Michael McClure, and Allen Ginsberg) who had read at the Six Gallery poetry reading in October 1955 that ushered in the West Coast Beat literary movement. I became enthralled with the literature of the Beat Generation, a phrase coined by Jack Kerouac eight years earlier, and a culture of practice in which I felt mostly at home—except that I was in a city and missed the countryside.

As time wore on, I lived both in Big Sur and in Marin County, where I made friends with whom I would ingest peyote, a small cactus plant native to the Chihuahuan Desert, which opened my mind to the sacred nature of our planet. On occasion, we would travel as a group to the north end of Pyramid Lake, north of Reno, Nevada, where we would build a fire in a cave Darrell Grover had found and hold our own version of peyote meetings through the night. In the morning, we would go skinny-dipping in the lake, where a hot spring emptied into the cool waters. We were a group of young men and women and kids (only the adults ate peyote), ridding ourselves of the taint of modern culture and investing ourselves with a sense of spiritual relationship with the Earth. High adventure in the Great Basin Desert, a vast empty landscape where one could roam free and listen to the wind.

Peyote greatly influenced me, opening me up to a sense of the sacred. The only other experience in my life that ever came close to peyote was life as a fire lookout camped atop a slab of sandstone surrounded by Ponderosa pine trees for a hundred days and nights a year beginning in the mid-1960s in northern New Mexico, where I would scan the forest for wisps of smoke that indicated a fire had broken out, where I would become one with habitat, where I would play my trumpet in concert with wild turkey and coyote, all of us performing a jazz sonata as part of the chorus of wildlife.

In 1961, when I was still in Marin County, Jimmy Hopper and Randy Allen joined us at Larkspur, in the foothills of Mount Tamalpais, for Christmas dinner. We smoked some pot, ate well, and decided that it was time to head toward New Mexico, which I had passed through in 1958 when hitchhiking across America. New Mexico had laid claim to me. I couldn't get it out of my mind. The Colorado Plateau and environs are a paradise of canyons, piñon-juniper grasslands, ponderosa pine forests—red-rock country that was home to ancestral Indians for millennia. The Intermountain West, that arid landscape between the Rocky Mountains to the east and the Cascade-Sierra Mountains to the west, beckoned me to explore it, to go adventurin', to run its waterways, to sleep beneath the stars.

In 1962, some of us began to trickle into New Mexico. Jimmy and Randy got gigs at the Three Cities of Spain in Santa Fe, where they played and sang folk music. I got a gig as a waiter and sometime bouncer in Claude's Bar. Claude, a lesbian who loved to sing, became a dear friend to me. One night she came to the bar in a beautiful gown (her normal garb was trousers, shirt, and sport jacket). As the evening progressed, she signed to the piano player that it was time. She sang her

Folk musician Randy Allen jamming with Jimmy Hopper, Santa Fe, 1970s. Photo by Seth Roffman.

Top: *Reno Kleen Myerson and Steve Samuels building a tipi, northern New Mexico, 1967. Photo courtesy of the Lisa Law Production Archives.*

Bottom: *John Kimmey and family near Llano, 1970s. Photo by Seth Roffman.*

favorite song, "La Vie en Rose." As she finished, the crowd cheered her on, except for one slightly wasted gent who put her down for wearing a gown, for being a lady. She put her cigarette out in his ear, and I ushered him out into the cool of evening on Canyon Road.

John and Marie Kimmey came to town, and John founded the American Church of God, a chapter of the Native American Church. Eventually they opened an alternative school, and later they would move to Arroyo Hondo, north of Taos. Peter Ashwandan came to town and distinguished himself as a master illustrator for such books as John Muir's classic *How to Keep Your Volkswagen Alive: A Manual of Step by Step Procedures for the Compleat Idiot.* I had sold John the VW that he used for his book. In Rolf Cahn's presence, John told me that Rolf, a fellow musician, had been the "compleat idiot" for whom the book was written. I once bought a bass viol for 125 pesos from John that he said he had played while performing with the great cornetist Muggsy Spanier.

By the late 1960s, many in our Marin County community had migrated to the Southwest. Rick and Sue Mallory moved to Mancos, Colorado. They were central to our early community and were among the finest people I have ever known. Dark Dick Brown already lived in Santa Fe and opened many doors to us. Alan and Joan Lober moved to Santa Fe and opened the Morningbird shop, which specialized in Indian artifacts and jewelry. For years the Lobers employed many of the Marin County gang of *peyoteros*. Yvonne Bond moved to New Mexico. She had grown up in California and had befriended many of the Beats in the Bay Area, among them Michael McClure.

Earlier in 1960, a Greek artist named Jean Varda, who lived on a barge/houseboat in Gate Five in Sausalito, invited us to go sailing on his beautiful sailboat. It was there that I met Stewart Brand, a skinny blond fellow newly graduated from Stanford University with a degree in biology. Over the next few years, Stewart and I became friends. At one point in 1963, Stewart invited me to join him in a project with the title America Needs Indians. Thus it was that my first wife Jean and I came to live in a forked-stick hogan at Navajo Mountain, Utah—the remotest part of the Navajo Reservation—for several months. Stewart roamed Indian Country from top to bottom, while we remained in our hogan trying to absorb Navajo culture, though neither of us was an anthropologist or fluent in the beautiful and difficult Navajo language. I did learn a lot about Navajo life, and this experience made it clear to me that indigenous culture is largely shaped by habitat. This, I realized, is why America needs Indians: traditional Indians regard homeland as sacred. This realization has influenced the way I have since chosen to live my life. I had dropped out of a culture with which I was out of sync, a culture where success was measured in terms of money, where consumerism was the reason to be, a culture now the militarily mightiest in the world,

Early peyoteros including Linda Ross, Jack and Jean Loeffler, Beth Dickey, Rick Mallory, Peter Ashwandan, David Melville, Dick Brown, a Ute Indian roadman, Tahiti Gervais, Robin Melville (holding Nava), Jimmy Sparrowhawk, Sue Mallory, Little Linda, and Teddy Harris, 1965. Photo by Stewart Brand.

a culture driven to secularize habitat and turn it into money by mining its minerals, developing the land with little or no regard for the landscape or its denizens.

It was the following summer, in 1965, that my wife and I first became fire lookouts in the Jicarilla Ranger District of the Carson National Forest in northwestern New Mexico. We manned the lookout from mid-April till late July. On July 3, 1965, late in the afternoon, Stewart Brand and Lois Jennings arrived in their VW bus from San Francisco. Steve and Barbara Durkee and their daughter Dakota, known as Koby, arrived in their van from New York. They were all expected. Unexpectedly, Jimmy Hopper, John Kimmey, and Dick Brown showed up from Santa Fe. We decided to have a peyote meeting. Everyone except Lois and me sat in a circle around the fire and ate peyote through the night. Lois abstained because she was the daughter of an Ottawa shaman and peyote was not part of her cultural lifeway; I abstained because I was a conscientious fire lookout.

The following morning was Koby's birthday, and her parents, Steve and Barbara, asked me to baptize her. I dipped my eagle feather in water from a nearby spring, combed Koby down from top to bottom, and pronounced her a Human Be-in.

The Durkees moved to New Mexico the following year and over time located the land north of Taos where, with help from Jonathan Altman, they founded the Lama Commune, which endures to this day. Barbara Durkee's brother, Hans von Briesen, known as Siddiq, and Sylvia Rodríguez, a high school girl from Taos, both helped build the first structures to be raised at Lama. Both went on to successful careers as respected educators.

In January 1966, Stewart Brand, Ken Kesey, and Ramon Sender Barayón produced The Trips Festival at Longshoreman's Hall in San Francisco. This was the very first of the great hippie gatherings that graced San Francisco over the next few years. It featured light shows, performances by the Grateful Dead and Big Brother and the Holding Company. LSD-laced punch elevated the consciousness of thousands of attendees. Some regard the Trips Festival as the preeminent bridge between the Beat scene and the hippie scene. It was a fireball of hippie consciousness that later transmogrified into enormous hippie gatherings in San Francisco such as the Human Be-In in January 1967, just before the Summer of Love. A related hippie moment occurred a few years later in New York State at the Woodstock Festival.

By the mid 1960s, Stewart Brand was deeply engaged in his great enterprise, soon to be published as *The Whole Earth Catalog*, which became the basic minimum-technology handbook for an entire generation of counterculturalists. The catalog won a National Book Award in 1972.

The Haight-Ashbury became the hippie neighborhood of choice in San Francisco, while Taos County became a mecca for communards and back-to-the-landers in northern New Mexico. One of the greatest of the communards was a Beat poet and former jazz alto sax player named Max Finstein. Max was one of my first friends in New Mexico in 1962. We had both spent quality time in North Beach, and we both recognized that New Mexico was one of the planet's most beautiful and evocative

Max Finstein (far right) with Ron Caplan and David Gordon at New Buffalo. Photo courtesy of the Lisa Law Production Archives.

Little Joe Gomez in Arroyo Hondo inspecting a slide photo of himself, 1973. Photo by Seth Roffman.

landscapes. Max teamed up with a young man from Pennsylvania named Rick Klein, who had come into an inheritance. Together Rick and Max founded the New Buffalo commune, one of the most celebrated of several communes in Taos County. After traveling to Israel to work on a kibbutz, Max returned to Taos County to help found the Reality Construction Company.

In an interview that I conducted with Rick Klein in 2008, he talked about New Buffalo.

> I was going to be a literature professor, and then I took LSD and saw that there's more to it than just this. There's being with your friends. Culture was very exciting at that time. I had an inheritance, and I bought land in New Mexico and got involved in New Buffalo. The first thing we did was have a peyote meeting, and Max [Finstein] was the roadman. Ultimately, I got very involved with Little Joe Gomez from the Taos Pueblo, with his brother John and all those old men up there. The last one just passed away last year. He was a hundred years old. . . . They were all exceptional people.

A young man named Arty Kopecky moved to New Buffalo, where he remained for seven years working the farm. He went on to write two books about his tenure there, *New Buffalo: Journals from a Taos Commune* and *Leaving New Buffalo Commune*, both introduced by actor/anarchist/author Peter Coyote and published by the University of New Mexico Press.

Situated at the western base of the Sangre de Cristo Mountains, a major range of the southern Rockies, Taos lies east of where the Río Grande bisects the vast sagebrush plain, creating a sense of space where anything wonderful is possible. This landscape, as seen from the side of Lama Mountain, was regarded by D. H. Lawrence as one of the most beautiful in the world. The Taos Pueblo is an ancient Indian community of Tiwa-speaking people. For centuries, the village of Taos was a center where Hispanos, Comanche Indians, and others met to trade goods and hold fiestas. It was once home to Kit Carson, the controversial US Army Scout. Taos is beautiful and fascinating and not to be trifled with. It can lure you in or spit you out depending on the circumstances.

Just as the Bay Area had been a haven for bohemians long before the arrival of the Beats and hippies, so had Taos been an artist colony since the arrival of Mabel Dodge Luhan early in the twentieth century. At the urging of Tony Lujan, Mabel's Taos Pueblo husband, Mabel constructed a large adobe home just south of the Taos Pueblo that became a center for intellectual and artistic life for half a century. Her visitors included D. H. Lawrence, Jaime D'Angulo, Robinson Jeffers, Georgia O'Keeffe, Ansel Adams, and many other celebrated artists, writers, and thinkers.

That art colony endured and took on a life of its own even as Mabel grew old and infirm. A new generation of bohemians became part of the Taos milieu in the 1950s and early '60s with the arrival of spiritual wanderers Jay and Liz Walker, artists John DePuy, Rini Templeton, Malcolm Brown and his wife, the weaver Rachel Brown, and author/environmentalist Edward Abbey. Craig and Jenny Vincent had been in Taos since the early 1940s. He was an old-time communist, and she was a great folk singer. Craig founded a weekly newspaper, *El Crepúsculo de Libertad*, and hired Edward Abbey to be the editor. Ed was an avowed anarchist, and he and Craig had troubled chemistry.

It was during this time that billboards began to fall in New Mexico as the result of human volition. There were inklings of a new kind of activism responding to the corporate military industrial complex that America had spawned, a complex about which former President Eisenhower had warned his fellow Americans.

In Llano, not far from Taos, yet another mobile commune, the Hog Farm, settled in for a spell. Its charismatic founder, Hugh Romney, aka Wavy Gravy, moved it there from California. Wavy is a direct cultural descendant of Ken Kesey's Merry Pranksters. Wavy and Tom Law kept order at the Woodstock Festival in August 1969. Lisa Law became a well-known photo-documentarian of the celebrated hippie scene from coast to coast. Tom Law and Reno Kleen Myerson brought Yogi Bhajan to New Mexico. The Yogi set up an ashram near Española on land found by Bill Steen, who went on to become the business manager for the ashram for several years thereafter. The ashram is still there.

At Lama, the Durkees invited their old friend Ram Dass, formerly known as Richard Alpert, to join their commune. Ram Dass authored one of the great hippie publications, the very successful 1971 book *Be Here Now*, published by the Lama Foundation. Before he became Ram Dass, Alpert had worked with Timothy Leary at Harvard, and both lost their jobs because they had administered psychedelic drugs

John Kimmey and Tellus Good Morning, Taos, 1970s. Photo by Seth Roffman.

to students. In *Be Here Now*, Ram Dass wrote about being thrown out of Harvard: "Everybody, parents, colleagues, public, saw it as a horrible thing; I thought inside, 'I must really be crazy now.' . . . And yet, I felt saner than I'd ever felt."

Ram Dass went on to found the Hanuman Foundation, parodied by the novelist John Nichols in *The Nirvana Blues* (1981). An avowed Marxist, Nichols arrived in Taos in the late 1960s, just in time to witness the social upheavals that resulted from the arrival of the hippies and their conflicts with the resident Hispanos. His 1974 novel *The Milagro Beanfield War*, one of the great novels to emerge from New Mexico, chronicled and invigorated grassroots reaction to developers determined to capitalize on northern New Mexico's landscape. John Nichols remains an independent counter-culturalist quite different from the communards.

Dennis Hopper's 1969 film *Easy Rider* portrayed two hippie buddies (Dennis Hopper and Peter Fonda) who rode their motorcycles across America. The movie includes their visit to New Buffalo. Hopper became enamored of Taos and bought the Mabel Dodge Luhan house and guest house, where he lived for several years thereafter. His presence contributed to the aura of celebrity that permeated the Taos atmosphere.

It was also in 1969 that my friend Karl Kernberger and I set out to travel the length of *el camino real de tierra adentro*, from northern New Mexico to Mexico City. Karl and I were part of a loose band who called ourselves "The Four Brothers Adventure Company." We made many side trips off the camino, including one to San Miguel de Allende, where we stayed in the home of John and Eve Muir. Later, in Mexico City, we met Victor Fosado, owner of a gallery of contemporary and pre-Columbian Mexican Indian artifacts, some of which I purchased for the Center for Arts of Indian America. Victor invited Karl and me to visit his macrobiotic nightclub, where his avant-garde musical group would be performing that evening.

Karl had his cameras and I my tape recorder, and I recorded this novel group performing strangely beautiful music on contemporary and pre-Columbian musical instruments. Two of the members of this group performed as actors in *El Topo*, Alejandro Jodorowsky's classic 1970 cult film about a gunfighter's quest for enlightenment.

From there, Karl and I went into the mountains of Nayarit and Jalisco to the Huichol Indian village of San Andres de Cohamiata, where we camped for a month and witnessed the annual Huichol peyote fiesta. I learned an enormous amount about these *indios* and how their beautiful habitat had influenced their cultural evolution. I came to see them as an endangered species and to understand that the eradication of indigenous mind by a capitalist monoculture could toll the death knell for our species.

When we returned to Santa Fe, a group of us known as Earthlings United for Better Life (EUBL) held our first and last meeting at John Kimmey's Santa Fe Community School, New Mexico's first alternative school. It was there that I first met Tom Law and Reno Kleen Myerson. I also met Bill Brown, the chief historian for the southwestern branch of the National Park Service. Bill, Jimmy Hopper, John Kimmey, and I thereafter founded the Central Clearing House to look at environmental problem areas around the Southwest. Harvey Mudd gave us a generous grant. Bill Brown had heard on the Department of the Interior grapevine that an enormous coal mine was to be built at Black Mesa, a great landform sacred to both Hopi and Navajo peoples. Bill and I took off for Black Mesa and spoke with a few Indians in the area, who knew nothing of the impending strip mine.

In April 1970, I drove to the Hopi village of Hotevilla to speak with my wise friend David Monongye about what Bill and I had learned. David called for a meeting of traditional Hopi elders to be held the following day on Second Mesa. I told what I knew, that the strip mine would be located in the heart of Black Mesa, that water would be pumped at the rate of 2,000 gallons per minute from the Pleistocene aquifer that lay below in order to slurry coal to a power plant near Bullhead City, Nevada, and that the rest of the coal would be shipped via an as-yet to-be-constructed railroad across the Kaibito Plateau to a soon-to-be-constructed, coal-fired electrical generating station near the southern shore of Lake Powell.

The Hopis were outraged that their tribal council, then chaired by Clarence Hamilton, would dare to sign contracts with the US government to result in this

Jack Loeffler distributing material about the Black Mesa strip mine at the Gallup Indian Ceremonial, 1971. Photo by Terrence Moore.

great sacrilege to their sacred homeland. The traditional Hopis, represented by David Monongye and Mina Lansa, asked me to help them make their case to the American public. On April 10, 1970, just twelve days before the very first Earth Day, Jimmy Hopper, Bill Brown, and I founded the Black Mesa Defense Fund. We were soon joined by photographer Terry "Más" Moore and thereafter by a small band of concerned citizens, and we worked as hard as we could for two and a half years to try to thwart the strip mining, but we ultimately lost to the Central Arizona Project. The corporate world and the political machine had conjoined, and it would take more than a handful of hippies to stop them.

In 1968, on a day off from my fire lookout, I found a new book in a small book-store in Durango, Colorado. The author was Edward Abbey, a guy I'd met in Claude's Bar in Santa Fe several years before. I recognized his picture on the dust jacket. The book was entitled *Desert Solitaire*. It was one hell of a read, and I realized that Abbey was a kindred spirit. A couple of weeks after we opened the Black Mesa Defense Fund, I found him on his fire lookout on the North Rim of the Grand Canyon. John DePuy was there visiting him, as was a woman named Ingrid. That evening, Ed and I took a walk, the first couple of miles of thousands of miles that we would hike over the next decades. I told him about the Black Mesa strip mine, the Navajo Generating Station, the whole sorry mess. By the end of the evening, we both had fires in our bellies that no six-packs of beer would ever quench. We were at war.

Top: *David Monongye at his home in Hotevilla, Third Mesa, Hopi Independent Nation, Arizona, 1970s. Photo by Seth Roffman.*

Bottom: *John Kimmey and David Monongye, 1970s. Photo by Seth Roffman.*

Ed Abbey followed his own convictions even if they went beyond the law. Suffice it to say that we fought those gangsters who tore up the landscape, who stole huge quantities of water, and who laid spiritual and physical waste to two beautiful indigenous cultures—all in the name of economic progress. And there were others who fought the good fight, almost to the death. I think here of the Black Mesa Defense Fund, of EarthFirst!, of Greenpeace, of the Big Mountain Support Group, and many others who shall go unnamed.

Here was a cadre of counterculturalists composed of artists, writers, musicians, intellectuals, outdoors people—activists all against the corporate/political hierarchy that had the nerve to call *us* ecoterrorists.

My great friend Edward Abbey was the spiritual leader of the modern radical environmental movement. The term *counterculture* does not come close to defining this multifaceted movement, still actively fomenting.

When Edward Abbey died, on March 14, 1989, four of us took our fallen comrade to a remote desert and buried him in his sleeping bag as he had requested. We loaded him into the back of my pickup truck, and as we started across an arroyo, we got stuck in the sand. Never in our scores of camping trips together did Ed and I fail to get stuck in mud, sand, or quicksand. On his last journey through his beloved Southwest, we got stuck yet again, only this time Ed couldn't help us get unstuck. But he had a good excuse.

Gary Snyder was one of five poets featured at the Six Gallery in 1955. Born in San Francisco, he grew up in rural Washington. Of his parents he said, "My father was involved in an organization called the League of Unemployed Voters . . . and he also did some union organizing work. . . . My mother was clearly and outspokenly anti-religious, anti-churchgoing, highly critical of dogmatic Christianity." Gary learned to do farm work as a youngster, graduated from Reed College, was a mountain climber and backpacker, and documents his extraordinary life in poetry.

Although Gary Snyder associated with the Beat poets, his poetry is far more in tune with nature. When he shared his cabin on the side of Mount Tamalpais with Jack Kerouac and Allen Ginsberg, he introduced them to a more Nature-oriented perspective. Deeply interested in anarchist thought, he has been influenced by Pyotr Kropotkin, the turn-of-the-twentieth-century philosopher exiled from Russia after the revolution.

Gary Snyder remains deeply interested in indigenous cultures and their relationship to home habitat. He became a Zen Buddhist in his youth and reads both Chinese and Japanese. Gary has contributed tremendously to the bioregional perspective. His essay "The Four Changes" has especially influenced the counterculture movement. He has been an enduring presence in the movement for over sixty years, as well as one of America's great poets. His book of essays *The Practice of the Wild* offers an

Left: *Edward Abbey with shotgun, 1980s. Photo by Terrence Moore.*

Right: *Gary Snyder and Stewart Brand, 2009. Photo by Jack Loeffler.*

enlightened view of humanity's place in Nature. He and Edward Abbey never met, but they were well aware of each other and shared a mutual respect. Their contributions to modern culture are profound. Great intellect alone is "insufficient unto the day." It takes great perseverance to reshape cultural perspective.

The entirety of the 1960s and '70s was fraught with cultural unrest. I was playing jazz in Indianapolis briefly in 1960. In the main I was honored to play with black musicians, and the Black Panther movement was coming into its own, which made for many intense moments. The Black Panthers contributed greatly to the civil rights movement, and Martin Luther King was making enormous headway bugging bigoted bureaucrats, including Orville Faubus, a governor of Arkansas who had invoked the National Guard to keep nine black students from attending Central High School in Little Rock in 1957. The renowned jazz bass player Charlie Mingus wrote a jazz chart entitled "Fables of Faubus," which is one of the hardest swingin' charts of the era. Dannie Richmond played drums with Mingus for many years. Together, Mingus and Richmond composed one of the greatest rhythm sections of all time. They helped kick America into awareness of the racial inequalities that persist even to this day.

Before English Pilgrims landed at Plymouth Rock, Massachusetts, in 1621, a huge entourage of colonists led by Juan de Oñate had settled near the confluence of the Río Grande and Río Chama in what is today north-central New Mexico. The year was 1598, and the colonizing entourage comprised Spanish, Basque, Moorish, Sephardic, and other peoples seeking a new way of life. Over four centuries later, Hispano culture is deeply rooted in the Southwest; it is rich in history, tradition, and wisdom about the land. Gradually, much Hispano culture has been subsumed by the ever-growing monoculture of the rest of the continent, but a strong countercultural force had its genesis in the New Mexico Hispano culture. Hispano culture itself is a crystal of many facets that include lowriders, the Alianza Federal de Mercedes led by Reies López Tijerina, the Brown Berets, and la Academia de la Nueva Raza. Established by Tomás Atencio, a native of Dixon, New Mexico, la Academia comprised scholars, artists, writers, musicians—all activists who used their collective talents to reinvigorate a sense of cultural identity in their homeland. One of New Mexico's great scholars in this tradition is Enrique R. Lamadrid, who grew up in Dixon and has used his many talents to nurture *querencia*, a deep and abiding love and recognition of one's place in homeland, a concept that does not have an English-language equivalent.

One of the great songs to emerge from this countercultural perspective is "Se Ve Triste el Hombre" composed by Cipriano Vigil. This song reflects the profound sadness experienced by many Nuevomexicanos that their land grants, forests, and waterways were taken from them by US government agencies. "My Name Is Popé," a poem by la Academia's own E. A. "Tony" Mares, tells the tale of how Popé, a Tewa-speaking Indian from Ohkay Owingeh, led a great revolt against the Spanish settlers in 1680, driving them out of New Mexico for twelve years.

In 1968, the American Indian Movement (AIM) was formed to fight social injustice and land rights violations against Indian peoples.

While much of AIM was carried out in the northern plains states, southwestern Indians became involved in response to the strip mining of Black Mesa in northern Arizona. Indians from throughout North America joined the effort, especially when the US Congress pitted Navajos and Hopis against each other in a dispute that resulted in the relocation of thousands of Navajos from their traditional homelands on Big Mountain, the southern extension of Black Mesa.

Throughout America, myriad subcultures rose to the surface to fight for social justice and preserve withering habitats. People of different cultural persuasions discovered a burgeoning unity of spirit. Native American scholar Vine Deloria wrote *Custer Died for Your Sins*. César Chávez and Dolores Huerta cofounded the National Farm Workers Association, which became the United Farm Workers. Edward Abbey wrote *The Monkey Wrench Gang*. Carlos Castañeda wrote *The Teachings of Don Juan*. Filmmaker Godfrey Reggio produced the Qatsi Trilogy. Musician Peter Rowan wrote "Panama

Red" and "The Free Mexican Air Force." These outlaw artists helped invigorate a new system of ethics embodied in Timothy Leary's slogan "Turn On, Tune In, Drop Out."

Counterculture wasn't all peace, balance, and harmony. Parents lost track of children who had turned on, tuned in and dropped out, sometimes to oblivion. Drugs wiped out previously wonderful minds and spirits. Jimi Hendrix, Janis Joplin, and Jim Morrison all died of drug overdoses within a year of each other, each of them just twenty-seven years old. But in spite of the downside of the counterculture, it led to a new level of consciousness and mindfulness that continues to permeate American and even global culture.

Almost a century before the Beat literary movement, Walt Whitman penned a phrase that spoke to many Americans: "TO The States, or any one of them, or any city of The States, *Resist much, obey little*; Once unquestioning obedience, once fully enslaved; Once fully enslaved, no nation, state, city, of this earth, ever afterward resumes its liberty" ("Walt Whitman's Caution," *Leaves of Grass*, 1900).

The father of young Ed Abbey read many of Whitman's verses to young Ned, as he was known. Years later, Abbey would use Whitman's words to further his own brand of anarchism by insisting that we *Resist Much, Obey Little*. Few of us have Abbey's strength of character. Could you resist the enslavement of modern media by shooting the screen of your television set? Ed realized the degree to which modern American culture had settled comfortably into consumerism.

Abbey lived simply and frugally his entire life. His fellow writer and philosopher Gary Snyder took simplicity a step further by moving into the forested wilds of the Sierra Nevada, where he built his simple home heated by firewood that he himself cut. He eased himself off the grid by installing solar panels with an accompanying system of batteries to provide what electricity he required.

These two men stand as leaders of the counterculture that remains embedded in contemporary society. The face of counterculture has changed since the man in the grey flannel suit was first juxtaposed with the bearded hippie. Many of today's lifestyles began a half century ago when the counterculture was new. Food, for example, is now the subject of careful scrutiny by consumers who insist on organically grown fruit, vegetables, meat, dairy products, and candy bars. My old friend Gary Paul Nabhan, a highly regarded ethnobotanist who cofounded Native Seed Search over three decades ago, has since become a prime mover in modern attitudes toward food. He has contributed to understanding the significance of pollinators and is also a great defender of the rights of indigenous peoples.

Shelter has become more efficient over the last half-century thanks to Lloyd Kahn's Shelter Publications and Bill and Athena Steen's Canelo Project.

Hair has long been associated with the hip population. Fifty years ago while still a fire lookout, I was told by my boss, the forest ranger in charge, to shave my beard on the grounds that it was a fire hazard. Today, half the working force of the US Forest Service wear beards. The other half are women, who have come into their own as archaeologists, rangers, and Forest Service supervisors—a change that is also part of the counterculture.

Although we have gained many footholds in various cultures of practice, including the arts and humanities, the civil rights movement, the antiwar movement, the environmental movement, and various spiritual disciplines, we are losing ground, not just as a counterculture movement but as a species within the planetary biotic community. Since the movement began in its current incarnation around 1960, the human population of the planet has more than doubled, the planet's resources have dangerously dwindled, and the climate itself is poised to change during the course of this century. Children born today will die in a far different world than the one into which they were born. Not only will climate instability prevail and global warming affect every corner of the planet, but also the human species may well be forced to turn against itself, to compete for what resources remain available—unless . . . unless . . . unless . . .

It has been well over half a century since I first came to northern New Mexico, now my beloved homeland. I had a sense of rebellion that I have never outgrown, but I trust and hope that I've evolved into a practitioner who continues to work for the well-being of homeland and its denizens regardless of species. I resist the interloper, the carpetbagger, the exploiter, in whatever guise one may appear, all the while realizing that I myself am an interloper, having blown in like a tumbleweed many years ago.

Intellectually I am pessimistic, but intuitively I am optimistic. One of the joys of living in this exquisite homeland is to sit of a winter's evening well bundled against the cold and look into that spot the breadth of a hand span and a half beneath the constellation Cassiopeia, where with my naked eye I can see what looks to be a star but is in reality the galaxy we call Andromeda. Just think of that! That galaxy lies some two and a half million light years from Earth and is home to an estimated 1 trillion stars, or more than double the number here in our own Milky Way. According to cosmologists, in 3.75 billion years or so, that distant galaxy and our own will merge or collide as the case may be. There are at least 100 billion other galaxies in the observable universe. That's roughly one galaxy for every human being who has ever lived.

Our solar system has spawned not only life but also at least one life form capable of evolving consciousness. It is profoundly sad to think that a species with our capacity for consciousness would squander such an opportunity. It doesn't have to end so ignominiously. Rather, we can look at ourselves yet again relative to this home habitat and discern which of our characteristics and pursuits run counter to the continuum of life as we know it. Let's use the new digital media that we're spawning to help foster a more compelling system of ethics, to reeducate ourselves into a new system of standards, invigorate cultures of practice that are not only viable but also celebratory of the miracle of existence, and then muster both individual and collective self-discipline to proceed in beauty.

Yvonne Bond, 2016. Photo by Jack Loeffler.

2

Yvonne Bond's Tale

AS TOLD TO JACK LOEFFLER

WHEN I WAS IN HIGH SCHOOL, I met Sterling Bunnell. I met him through friends of friends of my brother's, actually. Sterling Bunnell was a turning point in my life. He fit right in with the North Beach activities I was doing. He was a medical student at the time at UC Medical School in San Francisco. He was about twenty-five. I was sixteen. Sterling was a very unusual person, came from a very unusual family— father a famous hand surgeon. They lived in a Victorian house in San Francisco that was at the top of Pacific Heights. It was like an aerie out of an Edgar Allan Poe story. Sterling and his father were naturalists, amateurs but very high-quality amateur naturalists. He knew a lot about birds and everything else.

So Sterling gave me a feeling for nature that was at once scientific and ecstatic, spiritual. And it was wonderful. He also was a falconer, and I used to go with him when he took his birds out to fly, which was an incredible experience. So we would go look at birds and bugs and everything there was to look at. He also introduced me to artists and poets and painters who lived in North Beach, including Michael McClure. We went to some fabulous parties at Michael McClure's in the late 1950s and early '60s. One time Jack Kerouac was there. He was in his cups with wine in the kitchen. I think it was just after *On the Road* had made its huge success and he was taking a dive at that time.

Then some of us, including darrell grover [who always used lower case for his name] and Mike and Joanne McClure and probably Sterling, went down to Big Sur and went to the house where Henry Miller was staying. Henry wasn't there. We talked to a woman there. We went to a cabin where we were supposed to meet Jack Kerouac, but he wasn't there and didn't show up.

Through Sterling I also met a psychiatrist named Mike Agron, who was very important in that scene. He was a great patron of the arts, of the Batman Gallery, I think, in San Francisco, which showed people like Bruce Conner.

While I was there at Berkeley, I went into the Kroeber anthropology library and read a lot of anthropology, including dissertations and papers about southwestern Native

American people, Mexican Indians. I spent a lot of time there. I wouldn't have put it this way at the time, but I was interested in the knowledge of nature and the spiritual connection to nature that indigenous cultures have and in absorbing however much of that worldview that I could as a non-native person.

At the same time I was also spending a lot of time with darrell grover. I met darrell in the late 1950s through Sterling. Darrell was essentially half Native American. He was a quarter Cherokee on one side of his family and a quarter Eastern Sioux on the other side, Lakota or Dakota. He was dark, he had straight hair, really dark brown piercing eyes. He could walk on the earth like no one I've ever seen. He wore only moccasins, very sturdy. He didn't wear boots or anything like that. He was extremely well read. He was reading all the time. He had tons and tons of really interesting books. He hadn't gone to college; he went for a while to the California College of Arts and Crafts. He was a working-class guy. He always worked in industrial plants of various kinds. Union guy, very leftward-leaning politically. First the Old Left, then the New Left.

He took me to public meetings in the East Bay of the actual Communist Party, the old Communist Party of the USA. Party meetings and jazz clubs were the first places I ever saw black and white people together, black and white couples, black and white people hanging out together in a social way that was comfortable, and it looked like they had been doing that for a long time and it was a good scene for them. Then darrell became involved in the New Left and I became involved in that too. I did sit-ins with SNCC [Student Nonviolent Coordinating Committee] and CORE [Congress of Racial Equality] more than fifty years ago. We sat in at Woolworth's lunch counter in Berkeley and a Cadillac dealership in San Francisco which would not hire black salespeople.

At the same time darrell introduced me to many of his friends, like Rick and Sue Mallory at Gate 5 in Sausalito. Rick's daughter Karen lived with them, and she was around the same age as Sue's daughter Marcella. They were around seven or eight when I first met them. Sue also had an older son named Teddy. Together, Rick and Sue had a daughter, Star, when they went down to live in a tiny cabin with a giant stone chimney deep in the trees in Bixby Canyon. So there were those four wonderful kids.

And Thad and Bev Thomas, also out at Gate 5. These were some people with some real soul to them, just incredible storytellers, raconteurs, a lot of life experience. They'd been to Mexico. They knew how to raise children naturally, more wholesomely and healthily than our generation. They camped a lot. They had beautiful, wonderful children and many beautiful, wonderful friends. They lived very simply, close to the earth. At Gate 5 they lived in rickety houseboats where you had to walk along these planks to get there and there were many wires strung for the electricity. Gate 5's not like that anymore from what I hear. This was in about 1959, '60, '61.

At the same time I met Jimmy Hopper, and I will tell you a little bit about these people. Rick Mallory was a skinny, intense guy. Came from a family that was kind of wealthy, and his stepfather was Robert Ruark, the columnist. Ruark, I guess, was kind of a bully who said, "You gotta be a man, you gotta be a man, Rick." Rick's real first name was Enrique. So Rick learned to box, became a Golden Gloves boxer. Had a few marks on his face that told that. He was also a stonemason and just a guy you could sit around the fire with and hear a lot of stories. For a nineteen or twenty year old, that was great.

Jimmy was more around my age, a young guy. Thad and Bev Thomas were a little older, like Rick and Sue. Thad was a painter in a kind of Gulley Jimson mode [Gulley Jimson is the artist protagonist of Joyce Cary's novel *The Horse's Mouth*], great big huge paintings with almost always a bright sun in the middle. They had about three little kids. Thad was famous for his homegrown. He was also famous for taking his TV by the cord—he was a massive man—and swinging it around and around and around till he had enough momentum to heave it out through the window of his houseboat into the bay.

Sue Mallory was from the Gump family in San Francisco who owned Gump's, a high-end store that sold beautiful artifacts from all over the world. She was an arch, haughty, very funny and warm woman who would look down her nose and had this excellent education, very well read, and also was part Native American and later changed the spelling of her name to Sioux. She was a little bit rotund, not really fat, but I think she was a little self-conscious about that. She always wore skin-tight black pants with usually a Mexican shirt. Sue's dad, Bob Gump, eventually joined us on some of our adventures, like to Pyramid Lake, and he spent a lot of time living in Mexico. He was a pretty hip, cool guy.

Sue was like a wonderful mother to all of us and Rick was like our dad and they were like our family. They cooked for us, we spent time with them, we camped with them, we traveled with them.

We were in darrell's kitchen in Blake Street in Berkeley and I was about nineteen years old, probably in my sophomore year at Berkeley. He said something like, "I know you want to get high. We're going to eat peyote and get away from the city, away from a lot of people, and into the country. It's Holy Medicine and people use it for healing." At that time we didn't know of any Native American Church meetings where we were. But darrell had read a lot about the peyote ceremony.

He said, "You want to stay away from any kind of speed, like methedrine. It will destroy the myelin sheaths on the nerve cells in your brain and you can become deranged. Stay away from heroin. Stay away from barbiturates. Pot's okay. Let's have the peyote first." So we ate the Holy Medicine at his house. He was my guide and the person who kept me safe, which was really important. He was about seven years older than I. The first time we ate Holy Medicine, we went to Marin County and went along the Coast Highway, and at a spot overlooking the ocean we stopped. I was really coming on, you know. I had eaten yogurt and some kind of berries, like raspberries, for breakfast. I got out of darrell's MG sports car and traipsed through some wet undergrowth and heaved up my yogurt and berries, and I just had to bow before it because I was looking at the Holy Spirit right there in front of me.

So we went back to the car and parked along the road so we could look down at the ocean, or so thought darrell. But I instead turned my back on the ocean and I was looking in complete wonder at the cars going by. I said, "Look, look at those space ships going by. They're just floating on air. Those people are floating by in these little capsules." I looked up at the steep hillside that was covered with brush and I could see that every plant species was a different shade of green. There were a thousand shades of green, and every plant had its own life, its own color, its own little niche place in the picture. That's when I really connected strongly with the spirit of nature and have never left.

To get back to the peyote days, I really want to emphasize that this is Holy Medicine. Some of us ate it on our own, without being in peyote meetings. Then we started having peyote meetings of our own, doing it as best we knew from having read books. There were no Native American peyote meetings that we knew of where we were. We tried to do things in the best way that we could and keep it all as clean and sacred, in our own way, as we could. Later on, some of our people became connected with Native American peyote meetings in Nevada. Eventually I went to many peyote meetings that had Native American people and non–Native American people.

John Kimmey was a man whom I'd met in Mexico in 1961 or '62. He had just gotten out of the Navy, and I remember he was from the Bay Area and he was going to Mexico City College. I had some friends who were going there. I lived in Mexico twice for six-month periods when I dropped out of college. I also lived in Boston for about three months. Kimmey and I were both jazz freaks, and he had some of the latest Coltrane records. We used to get together to listen to the weekly jazz program on Mexican radio that played all the latest records from the United States. I said to Kimmey, "I'm going back to the Bay Area. Why don't we get together out there? I've got some great friends and we eat peyote." We were talking about peyote which you could buy in the big *mercado* in Mexico City. He said, "Oh, that sounds great."

So I got back to the Bay Area and showed up at darrell's apartment on Blake Street in Berkeley. And there were Steve Elvin and Linda Ross. Somehow darrell had met them during the time I was in Mexico, where I had met John Kimmey. Then Kimmey came over too.

Linda Ross and I became good friends. The two of us spent a lot of time together on the road. We hitchhiked back and forth between Santa Fe and the Bay Area twice, with many incredible adventures. Linda Ross was a really good blues singer. She was about five-eight and a good 180 pounds or so. She had a very strong personality and was kind of fearless. Her size made her kind of imposing and I always felt safe with her. I was kind of quiet. She always wore almost all the clothes she had with her when we were hitchhiking, which was about three layers of long, colorful skirts, a whole bunch of jewelry, a pair of sandals, three shirts. My mode of dress was a red ban-danna, Levi jeans and a guy's Levi jacket, sandals or moccasins. This was in the early 1960s before the upsurge of hippies. Very few people had seen anything like Linda Ross and me on the road. I'd stand out there on the shoulder with my thumb out and she'd hide, and then she'd jump out when they'd slow down. We'd both get a ride. I was about twenty-two. We made our first trip to celebrate her twenty-first birthday. We carried little old raggedy Army surplus sleeping bags rolled up on top of our Army surplus backpacks, which had aluminum canteens of water and peanuts and raisins.

We all often went to a place called Pyramid Lake that darrell had found. Pyra-mid Lake is on the Paiute Reservation in Nevada. It's not too far from Carson City. It's the remains of an ancient inland sea that has the Truckee River feeding into it. White pelicans nest there. The water is extremely brackish. It has a kind of native trout called cui-ui. And there are tufa formations at one end, like out at Jemez Springs here in New Mexico. They were tall spires, called the Needles, at the northern end of the lake, which had fewer visitors than other parts of the lake. The Needles were pockmarked with holes from the underground hot springs that had over the centuries formed the Needles.

darrell and I were out there one time in about 1961 with his son, Orpheus Grover, who still lives out in California. Orpheus was about six years old at the time. We were walking around the needles and Orpheus said, "Look, Dad, here's a cave." We cleared the tumbleweeds away and then we could see the top of the entrance. Sand had piled up in the bottom part. There was a cave that had been inhabited. It was smoke-black-ened. It had a natural chimney from the inside to the outside. We spent the after-noon scooping out the sand. The cave was just big enough for ten or so people. Also, Pyramid Lake was the place where Wovoka started the Ghost Dance. Very, very holy place. Not many people went out there at that time except for fishermen, especially to the Needles area.

So our gang of Rick and Sue and their four kids, and darrell and Orpheus, and me and John Kimmey and Linda Ross and Steve Elvin and Jimmy Hopper and Jack Loeffler used to go out there. John soon met Marie and they got married. He proposed to her at Pyramid Lake. We ate Holy Medicine in the cave and had our own kind of meeting there, with darrell as the guiding force. We were certainly inspired by the many spirits that were there. On one of our first trips out there, not long after I had come back from a stay in Mexico, as we were driving up to the cave, we saw

American Church of God peyote elders, among them, Randy Allen, Dick Brown, Rosemary Brown, John Kimmey, Chris West, Yvonne Bond, Heather Kimmey, and Concha Allen, at Linda Pedro's home in Chimayó, ca. 2008. Photo by Jack Loeffler.

an eagle—can't remember if it was a golden or a bald eagle—land on a prickly pear cactus holding a wriggling snake in its mouth, just like on the Mexican flag. Our jaws dropped in unison.

In the cave, we could go way back in time and become ancient people, Stone Age people. In the morning we'd go down to the hot springs, which at that time bubbled up right at the edge of the lake not far from the cave. We just did this without clothes. We streaked ourselves with the rich brown mud in the springs and picked up little leathery puffballs that grew nearby. When they were squeezed, rust-colored spores would squirt out. That way we could poof dots on our bodies along with the mud stripes. One time I sat for hours by myself in the springs and watched a large butterfly slowly emerge from its chrysalis that was hanging on the edge of the bank.

So there we were out in the Stone Age, and fighter jets would come flying over from an air force base. Sometimes one would cut its engines and fly through in between the Needles and then pull up. Then there'd be a huge sonic boom. At that time there was also aboveground atomic testing still going on not that far from us.

We could come down—literally—back from Pyramid Lake to the Bay Area, all of us just glowing and feeling wonderful. The whole bunch of us would sit down in some little restaurant on the highway with our hair just sticking out from our heads full of brackish hot springs water, our cheeks just completely pink from the sun, and the little kids all running around freely. Some of us were dressed in Mexican peasant blouses with bare feet. The whole restaurant would fall silent.

I wouldn't have gravitated toward this kind of life that I had if it weren't for that Beat consciousness of "Hey, we're not going to work for the man, you know. We don't want to buy into this system. We don't want to buy into the military industrial complex. We want to be aware of the environment around us and enjoy it to the most and be aware of the people around us and of trying to do something good for the planet." So there were relatively few people at that time. The scene was pretty small. And the word "hippie" was kind of a bad word. It meant, like, a fake hipster kind of thing. By about 1966, just a few years later, there were a million hippies emerging and it wasn't a bad word anymore. There were thousands hitchhiking and turning on and playing music and hanging out and doing various kinds of consciousness raising.

The pure LSD that came along first was very good. I was fortunate to have some of the first doses of that with friends and then psilocybin from Mike Agron, the psychiatrist, who gave it to volunteers and then recorded our experiences. Believe it or not, the LSD came from a chemist called Light and Company in England, and some I think came from Sandoz, where Albert Hoffman worked. So we were very privileged to get that. Afterwards it started to become adulterated when it was out on the street, except for Owsley's lab in the hills of Berkeley, which made very good LSD. As with peyote, it lifted the veils from one's eyes so you could see that everything is moving and flowing all the time, everything is changing every second—that we're completely connected on an energetic level with everything and everyone and that every rock is alive.

I wanted to say a thought I had about the counterculture. This actually comes from a remark that was made by Noam Chomsky. Let me go back a little bit and say that many people think that the counterculture that came out of the 1960s may have been great or may have been not so great, but it kind of faded. We thought we wanted to change the world through the great music that was bursting forth in such abundance in those days, through political activity, through raising our consciousness, and so on. And it may be perceived that that didn't happen the way we wanted it to.

However, Noam Chomsky brought up an interesting point, and he's pretty certain about this. He says that the effect that it had was that it humanized the culture in general, and speaking specifically about the culture in the United States, but really the culture worldwide, wherever that kind of counterculture reached. I think I would have to agree. Like, more human values are seeping into things all the time, like putting human needs first, and by extension, the needs of all the creatures that we are interdependent with and live with and are part of. And our consciousness that was raised by means of being in nature, through sometimes taking substances, sometimes visiting with gurus or *curanderos* or whatever means we used to expand our consciousness, we became aware that there's really no separation between us and other creatures, between us and the flow of energy. And you can talk a lot about that flow of energy, Jack.

So take heart. The changes are ripening, and let's keep going.

At the age of twenty-three I was one of the national organizers for the Student Committee for Travel to Cuba. I was one of the West Coast organizers of the trip. We were going to Cuba to break the travel ban which had been imposed by the US government, saying that after the Revolution and Fidel Castro took hold, Americans could not visit there. China, North Korea, and North Vietnam were also on that list. Ours was the second trip and took place in 1964, and there were eighty-four of us. We spent two months in Cuba. It was great, actually. The music in Cuba is *fan*-tastic! And Cubans are very musical, very warm, very friendly people. They loved having us there because they had had so many American tourists for so long.

We got to play baseball with Fidel and Raul. We got to go to Carnaval in Santiago on the far eastern end of the island, which was incredible. It was a poor area, mostly black. There were almost no streetlights. There was a conga line that was as long as Santiago, that went in and out of everybody's house with people playing whatever they could lay their hands on, in da-dung-da-dung dung, da-dung-da-dung-da-dung rhythm. Just simply incredible.

We were also constantly in contact with a five-year-old turnover in the life and social structure and economics of an entire people [after the 1959 Cuban Revolution led by Fidel Castro] and saw change on every level. Artists' and dancers' cooperatives in fancy mansions. Little factories springing up that made refrigerators and light bulbs. There was so much enthusiasm for the Revolution at that time.

We got to see Che Guevara—I believe it was in a union hall—taking part in a debate. The topic was "Material Incentives versus Moral Incentives in the Revolution." And there was actual, thoughtful debate. Che was on the side of moral or ethical incentives.

When we arrived back in New York, there wasn't a very warm reception for us by the airport security. They snatched our passports out of our hands and stamped them Invalid. The leaders, including me, shortly thereafter got subpoenaed by the House Un-American Activities Committee to testify about how we snuck all those people to Cuba and where the funds came from. So I waited around in New York until our session with the committee in October. Pete Seeger had been before this group earlier, and other writers and artists and movie people. Rather than taking the Fifth Amendment like some others had before us, we got coached by this lawyer, and we learned to talk so that we wouldn't get busted for contempt but so that we could have a platform to say that we're not foreign agents, we're Americans, we disagree with policies of the government and would like to see change, we think we can speak up for that.

After I went to Cuba, I came back to the Berkeley-Oakland area and got involved in the 1964-65 Free Speech movement that happened at UC Berkeley when the campus authorities tried to shut down one of the tables at Sproul Gate that various political organizations, both left and right, manned. A lot of discussions took place at those tables. The student response was strong and big. Here's a bit of what Mario Savio, one of the leaders, said.

> But we're a bunch of raw materials that don't mean to be made into any product! Don't mean to end up being bought by some clients of the University, be they the government, be they industry, be they organized labor, be they anyone! We're human beings! . . . There's a time when the operation of the machine becomes so odious—makes you so sick at heart—that you can't take part. You can't even passively take part. And you've got to put your bodies upon the gears and upon the wheels, upon the levers, upon all the apparatus, and you've got to make it stop. And you've got to indicate to the people who run it, to the people who own it, that unless you're free, the machine will be prevented from working at all.

That all merged into the Vietnam Day Committee, because the war in Vietnam was really ramping up in the mid sixties. I was one of many organizers. The antiwar demonstrations had started small and grew to a hundred thousand people marching en masse through Oakland and Berkeley down the main thoroughfares. At one point we had the Hell's Angels as kind of monitors. That got to be a little hairy. I will never regret that I helped get that many people out against the war, handing out leaflets that I and others had written and run off on those old Gestetner clank-clank machines down in a basement somewhere.

In the group I belonged to, the Progressive Labor Party, darrell and I grew disenchanted with their very rigid point of view. They thought the revolution was around the corner, which we didn't. And it wasn't. I myself couldn't take their increasing espousal of violence. So we dropped out. darrell was growing his hair and beard longer and longer and wearing a tan suede jacket with very long fringe.

And I came to New Mexico in 1966. I stayed in Santa Fe for '66, '67, '68, and part of '69. On a trip to California, I became very ill and ended up staying there for three and a half years. That was the three and a half years when there were a lot of demonstrations, uprisings in cities, fights between people and the police, university sit-ins. I was in Berkeley, although I was sick in a house, unable to go out much for six months.

Helicopters flew over and dropped tear gas on the Berkeley campus on a regular basis. I think it was in Berkeley that the famous picture was taken of a demonstrator putting a flower in the barrel of a gun of a national guardsman.

So I was getting burned out. Another thing that was happening that was very negative at that time was that . . . so many of us had taken things like LSD in the early days. These drugs were becoming commonly available as street drugs and were sometimes quite adulterated, so you really didn't know what you were getting. Many people were also starting to turn to the dark side and take things like speed and barbiturates, narcotics. There were many, many AWOL soldiers in San Francisco. I'll never forget that. You'd see them wrapped in their little army blanket with a buzz cut and just walking around. They'd deserted.

So it got pretty chaotic, kind of dangerous, and I didn't like the vibes in the big city any more. And I really wanted to come back to New Mexico. When I got on my feet, I did. I came back here and what I had in mind was "I just want to have a garden and live simply." I've lived here ever since. When I came back in '73, I stayed with Karl Kernberger. That's when I saw you again, Jack, and Kathy, whom you'd gotten together with, and got restarted on my life here.

The first time I lived in Mexico City, in 1961, I lived with Daniel Moore, who is a poet and artist I had met at UC Berkeley. The second time, in 1962, was really remarkable in that I stayed with the artist Bruce Conner and his wife, Jean Sundstedt Conner, who was pregnant at that time with their son Robert. This was an incredible scene. I was twenty-two. I barely knew them. I had seen them at a few parties, right? And I was down there in Mexico City. I knock on their door in Mexico City and say, "Hi! Do you think I could stay here for a while?" [*Laughs*] Now Bruce was a pretty eccentric guy, and Jean was very normal and calm. Bruce was, like, really hyper and skinny.

Without saying a word, Bruce grabs a roll of heavy plastic stuff like you'd put on your windows. He cuts off a swath of it and vigorously crunches it all into a big mass, gets a staple gun and throws this plastic down and staples it into the wood floor. Throws a blanket on it and puts a pillow on it and says, "There you go." That was the start of my six months of staying with Bruce and Jean. While I was there, we did stuff, like we visited every place in Mexico City that had murals by David Alfaro Sequeiros, who was a very left-wing muralist who was in jail at that time in Mexico. He created sculptural effects in his murals, which are extremely powerful and hard-hitting in depicting the sometimes dire conditions of the poor in Mexico. It was found in some major buildings, as well as places like electrician's unions. There were over a dozen venues that we all visited together.

We were also visited by a *curandero* whose name was Don Isauro Nava. How he got our address I'll never know. It was one of those magical moments. We're on the second or third floor and we were all sitting around. There's a knock on the door and there's a very diminutive Mazatec Indian man with a hand-woven bag over his shoulder, campesino clothing, who very softly and humbly says in Spanish, "I hear there are some people here who would like to have a mushroom ceremony." So we said, "Yes." And that was our first mushroom ceremony with Don Isauro Nava. Now this is getting to what you're saying about the knowledge of the indigenous people of their habitat.

Those present at our mushroom ceremony, which lasted all night, were me, Bruce and Jean, a Mexican middle-class couple maybe in their thirties whose name I forget, and Timothy Leary. Don Isauro Nava came with his helper, his nephew Bernardo. The helper would eat half a dose, whereas we all got the complete dose. And the helper would take care of us. You had to have somebody to take care of you. The ceremony took place at night. It was notable in that the Mexican couple, both the man and the woman, tried to jump out of the windows several times. We were on the second floor. These very diminutive Indian men had to try to physically restrain these much larger people, which took up a lot of the night.

Jean and Bruce Conner and Yvonne Bond, 1962. Photo courtesy of Yvonne Bond.

But as a result, Alan Russo, Steve Leiper, Beth Branaman—who had been married to Robert "Ronnie" Branaman, an artist—the four of us went to Huautla de Jiménez in Oaxaca, which was made famous in some writing, I think by Gordon Wasson, about mushroom ceremonies. Don Isauro Nava invited us there.

We traveled there by bus—big bus to littler bus and then the rattletrap bus with everyone carrying chickens, and then get out and walk from there. Huautla is in the Sierra Mazateca, which is quite steep and subtropical, the kind of place where dahlias were growing as a native plant. I can't remember if he met us or not or if we had a map. We got there about dusk. The people there were coffee growers, including Don Isauro and his family. He also had a milpa, a plot of corn, which was quite a way from his house up and down steep terrain.

So we arrive at his house. We were miles from the nearest store. The women all wore brightly embroidered *huipiles*, often with large representations of flowers and birds. Don Isauro and his wife were very warm and welcoming. They had a little kitchen covered with a ramada attached to the house. Next came what I think was a lesson. He asked us, "Would you like some cookies for a snack?" and we said, "Oh yes," thinking they had cookies around. Well, they didn't have any cookies. That meant that he had to walk miles to the nearest store and buy some cookies and bring them back hours later. I think that was saying, "Here's the extent to which we will go to welcome a guest into our midst. Take it seriously." And he had a bad back. It blew me away. Or maybe it was just an everyday thing for them, I don't know.

We had an incredible mushroom ceremony. He had a small terra cotta pottery bowl, and he sized each one of us up individually while he placed fresh mushrooms in the bowl that would be our individual dose. It was a bowlful of mushrooms. While we were there, he showed us some of the mushrooms growing from a pile of dung in the middle of a trail.

Don Isauro was very political. He had a shortwave radio. There was no electricity there. And he listened to radio stations all around the world. This is a guy who presents himself as a humble uneducated person. He wasn't. He was brilliant. He knew what was going on in the world.

It was pitch black inside the house at night. I think it was around new moon time. The mushrooms started to take effect, and Don Isauro sang and chanted, as I recall. I had developed a little rapport with Don Isauro in Mexico City because I spoke some Spanish. Now I was starting to see visions. In a soft voice I told Don Isauro what I was seeing. He was interested.

When the mushrooms had really taken effect, Don Isauro got really active. He impersonated or became several different beings, one of which was a mestizo Mexican singing a very sad and sentimental song. He perfectly became that person. At another point he jumped up and said, "Yo soy el aguila Mexicana!" [I am the Mexican eagle!] We're in the little dark room. You could hear the wings flapping and feel the breeze. We just sat there with our heads bowed as he flew around the room. This is where you're melting into everything. It was fresh psilocybin.

As I heard about other kinds of ceremonies with mind-altering plants, the aim was often to take you as far into the death experience as possible without you actually dying. It seems that is what Don Isauro was doing, though he never said that. I didn't know that beforehand. I had to go out and pee, so Bernardo lifted me up by the arm and took me outside and made sure I didn't fall down or wander away. I think it was during or just after that—it was completely dark outside—I felt that I had died and I was leaving my body. I lifted up out of my body and I said, "Oh wow, gee, I died so young. That's kind of a shame." I went higher and higher up in the sky and was flying along among the planets and stars. I thought, "You know, it's not that bad to have died here at this time. This is good, to have died here in Mexico." So I lifted up my arms and was going to keep going, happily soaring along. I kind of hear this little voice that says, "Come back, come back," and I go, "Oh, I guess it's time to come back in my body."

So I gradually drifted back there and settled back into the body, which I think was lying on the ground. I guess Bernardo lifted me up. It was a thousand-year journey in ten minutes or something. But I had the realization of life and death, and that has stayed with me the rest of my life.

When I came back, it was still very dark. We were getting deeper and deeper into the experience. Not too far before dawn, Don Isauro got a simple enamel candle holder that you could buy at a village mercado. It had a candle in it. He struck a match and lit the candle, and it looked like fireworks going off to us because we had been in the dark for so long. We just instinctively bowed down, and he was bowing and bowing before this flame. And he said, "Es la verdadera luz de Díos!" again and again. "It is truly the light of God."

He knew the plants, and he and other people there walked around with us and said this is this and that is that. We also ate *ololiuqui*, which was made from a morning glory species or two. We went to someone else's house, and they ground up this green mash and made almost like a shake out of it and we drank it. When you had that in you, everything turned green. It wasn't really a powerful high, but it was a subtle plant high.

We could see at the time that those people were just hanging on in that niche because of all the economic pressure against them. They had a working democracy going on in that place, except that it didn't include women as officers. But among the men, they had what they called a mayor that rotated I think every year. It seems to me that the mayor also served as the head of the local association of the farmers who grew coffee. They needed that because the coffee buyers who came through there were basically the thugs for large coffee companies who would literally brutalize the farmers to get the lowest price they could and sometimes kill them.

The people in that position of being the growers' representative had been assassinated before. What I heard, and I don't know if this was true or not, is that in years after we were there, Don Isauro was later assassinated himself. I don't remember how I heard that.

Also, Robin and David Melville went there several times for significant periods of time. Robin had her daughter Nava there, named after Don Isauro Nava. There was a big Mexico–San Francisco–New Mexico connection. Mexico was our India, and I think that's a good thing to say because so many of the East Coast people went to India. We went to Mexico to find the curanderos, the substances like magic mushrooms or psilocybin, the experiences, the backcountry people, the campesinos, the real deal.

So there you have both people being close to the earth and hanging on in their niche as best they can, given the economic pressures, given the soil erosion where they were growing their corn in steep locations—kind of a strong but marginal existence. I think there may have been tuberculosis there. I was out for a walk early one morning while I was there, and there's Bernardo leaning up against the door of his house looking kind of ill and coughing a lot and spitting out blood.

I often wonder if Don Isauro's children ended up picking lettuce in Salinas, in that sad scenario, and losing their knowledge of the plants of Oaxaca.

Peter Coyote, 2015. Photo courtesy of Peter Coyote.

3

We Know What to Do with Desire

PETER COYOTE

EVEN AN INTREPID SELF-REVEALER LIKE ME (an author of *two* memoirs) quails at the challenge of saying something fresh and insightful about the period between 1965 and 1975 we refer to as the Sixties. Its hopes, endeavors, and errors have been exhaustively chronicled, and the counterculture's collective offering of what "better" might look, feel, taste, and smell like has been iterated in every medium except perhaps scratch-and-sniff strips. At this point, the most useful approach might be to return to the ground level of that generational mind, speculate and generalize a bit to recapture something of the pre-LSD, pre-weed, pre-hormonal influences, aspirations, and assumptions that were the broth in which my generation was cultured. It is from this mix that the counterculture's Medusa-like writhing ball of snakes (and let me say that I revere serpents) was hatched. So for an imaginative review of some formative impulses and energies, let me revisit the era of World War II.

The United States was the triumphal victor of that conflict. We suffered neither the Russian sacrifice of blood (22 million) nor the bombing of our cities, factories, and infrastructure that had decimated Europe, from London east through Italy, and Japan. In astoundingly short order, our workers produced planes, tanks, trucks, weapons, and matériel to smother our enemies. The cultures of every country in Europe were integrated into our fighting forces, adding to our intelligence-gathering capabilities. Why should we not have been proud and arrogant? Our culture was sought after in every marketplace. Jazz, blues, swing, then rock 'n' roll; our blue-jeaned, antiauthoritarian, don't-fuck-with-me cowboy posture; our films and stars; our tuxedos and martinis. Our cars were wonders of engineering, style, and potential. The entire nation was wise-guy fresh and cocky.

This is the world I was born into in 1941. As we grew into social consciousness, my peers and I were steeped in television shows like *The Adventures of Ozzie and Harriet*, *Marcus Welby, M.D.*, and *Leave It to Beaver*. They delivered a world without shadows, a sunlit geography of guile-less innocence, where adults were sexless, wise, and kind and the gee-whiz kids were gently reprimanded for their faults until they effortlessly achieved the mindset of good Americans. No mention was made (to kids anyway) of post-traumatic stress disorder coursing through the returning veterans like a lethal gene. No mention of their having burned humans alive in the caves of the Pacific, roasting them with napalm, or firebombing major European cities like Dresden, whose not-necessarily-Nazi mothers, fathers, and children were transformed into smoke and sticky ash with the implacable reliability of the ovens at Auschwitz.

The British were admired for their pluck and graceful manners under incessant bombing, but few Americans appeared to connect the Brits' suffering to that of the hapless civilians in Europe and Japanese cities we razed to the ground. And yet, acknowledged or not, the blowback of the deeds required to survive a war percolated below the exuberant chop of daily life, surfacing in alcohol-fueled hazes, random scenes of domestic violence, and depression, all masked to some degree by the stultifying pursuit of material wealth.

While science and technology were constructing (and selling) a frictionless electronic future of perfect appliances and cars, lives of leisure supervised by machines and labor-saving devices (if you could afford them), many homes were shadowy places haunted by alcohol and sleeping pills, desperate women trying to understand the men who often ignored, belittled, or beat them and at times appeared to be only superficially domesticated.

My father and his friends drank heavily. They boxed (and in my dad's case, brawled) and followed prizefighting avidly until that bloody metaphor floated through them like an internal command. They were sharp eyed, alert, quick to take offense, and quick to settle things. No American would be "pushed around," and they responded to provocation as their fathers had, like my grandfather, fighting union organizers with a baseball bat when they tried to make an example of his factory and wrest it from his control.

For lucky others, many of whom had never served, postwar America was a feeding trough, with an endless supply of money. For quick-witted men like my father and his friends, opportunities to become rich abounded. The movies made before and after the war prepared the average Joe for the rise of a new democratized millionaire class, with high-spirited, joyful confections where Fred Astaire and Ginger Rogers or Cary Grant and Katherine Hepburn sizzled and romped in their elegant clothes and palatial homes, selling the lifestyles of the rich and famous long before the franchise ever appeared on TV and before Ralph Lauren discovered the trick of mass-marketing old-money style.

In homes with fewer resources, vets were taking advantage of government programs to further their education and buy homes. They had conquered the beasts of Europe and surely could conquer whatever petty obstacles peace time might toss in their path. But they were called on to work long and hard hours. Fathers were often absent and mothers stressed as sons like me grew into adolescence.

Emmett Grogan, Susan Grinel, Harvey Kornspan, Richard Brautigan, and Gene Grimm at an Artist Liberation Front meeting in Haight-Ashbury. Photo courtesy of the Lisa Law Production Archives.

My home was *not* like those TV families, and from what I later learned, neither were the homes of millions of other young people from Ohio and Nebraska, Kansas and Florida and all points east and west who fled to the Haight-Ashbury to take their chances in the wild San Francisco streets.

My own home, a minefield of terrifying outbursts, potential violence, and actual abuse—not sexual abuse, but threats, exhortations, dismissal, and corrosive denigrations of my capacities and capability—was paradise compared with the homes of young people I later met. While I thought my name was Stupid Son of a Bitch until I was thirteen or so, I met girls whose bodies had been covered by their fathers when their mothers walked in and turned around and walked out as if they had seen nothing. A friend of mine was hung upside down in an outhouse for eight hours for angering his stepfather. And there were many who suffered greater abuse.

They migrated to California, to New York's Lower East Side, to Minneapolis–St. Paul, to LA, arriving with a restlessness and hunger for unpaid promises coursing through them like a buried river; hungry for release and hungry, too, to receive their share of America's enticing promises, of which they had seen pitiably few. Where *was* this golden life we had been advertised into believing?

Before too long, youthful subcultures grew up around folk music and rock 'n' roll—aggregations of young people with nothing to do, some disposable income, and a deep yen to belong to something comprehensible and palpable. Bluegrass, rock 'n' roll, and blues were soon accompanied by marijuana, magic mushrooms, and LSD. Initiation into the secrets of these substances became the coded context of conversations by which members of this growing, disaffected guerrilla population might recognize fellow irregulars.

As this army gathered volunteers, it amassed ebullience and confidence. We developed vocabulary, art, and entertainments impenetrable to those who were not initiated into drugs and the ecstasies of rock and roll. When thousands of young men and women, participating in massive celebrations, became cognizant of their numbers, they developed confidence based on an exaggerated sense of their power and agency.

As we became visible, torqueing acceptable fashion and style into unrecognizable permutations and cultural references, sporting long hair that announced our freedom, we were not always alert to the subtle ways life can undermine hope. We brought with us the comforting certainties of our high-school civics classes concerning the way "things were supposed to work." We *knew* (we thought) what a democracy was. We knew how it was supposed to function, and now, feeling ourselves a new majority (wrong again), we felt that the time to express our will, to exercise our agency, and call in the nation's marker on issued promises—in short, to take over—was to occur in that historical moment.

Looking backward, it was perhaps this exaggerated sense of agency coupled with fundamental misunderstandings about how power actually (and has always) worked that led my generation to believe that we could remake the inheritance of the past into a future that we actually wanted and that we could do it in short order. We underestimated the ferocity with which the people who had clawed their way to power would kill and maim to retain it, even murdering their own children. We came together bonded by optimism, protected from certain consequences of our sexuality by the pill, introduced to radical philosophies and ideas by older bohemians. While we might not have agreed on precisely what kind of future we wanted, it was a fairly universal assumption in our vague counterculture models of how life should operate in our country that being an *employee* was very low on nearly everyone's list of personal desires, somewhere below syphilis.

My father often said to me, "A little knowledge is a dangerous thing." Because I interpreted his remark as simply another of his creative ways of informing me that he found me stupid, it never occurred to me that he might have been correct. Our imperfect knowledge of the greed, hatred, and delusion that shape the world, along with our imperfect awareness of our own muddy, contradictory intentions and desires, made us believe that we could create a world without shadows, a simpler, more understandable world in accordance with our simplistic understandings, better than the one we had failed to master as children.

Left: *Peter Coyote and banjo player J. P. Pickens in California.*
Photo courtesy of Peter Coyote.

Right: Peter Coyote in Olema, *1969. Photo courtesy of Peter Coyote.*

"Love is all you need" may sell a lot of records, but you can't eat it or talk yourself
out of pain if your lover decides that someone *else's* love is all they need. Loving red-
lined realtors and bigoted loan officers will not get your family a home if you happen
to have too much melanin in your skin. Love won't resolve egocentric desires to be in
charge, to be considered important, to be consulted in decisions about your life, and to
be the equal of those in power. Impulses like these coursed through the counterculture,
the communes, peace movements, the head shops, and hip merchandisers as readily as
they did through the hard-edged anarchist communities I inhabited, and all of them
mirrored what coursed through local governments and Washington. We did not fully
know ourselves, which is to say that we did not fully understand what being human
meant and required and that ignorance harnessed to youthful energy and confidence
was like driving a car at high speed with blacked-out windows, sometimes producing
toxic and destructive effects. These dangers fertilized the seeds of our old lives we'd
brought along with us, seeds that blossomed and choked naive hopes and promises.

I am making things sound bleaker than I actually feel, but this perspective is
a necessary corrective to self-congratulatory memories that fail to include sexual
disease, death by overdose and murder, and the careless spending of life's energies on
personal indulgence and occasional twaddle.

And yet some things must be said in gratitude for the extraordinary efforts,
diligence, and depth of conviction that my peers exhibited in pursuit of what we

Peter Coyote with Floyd Red Crow Westerman (middle). *Photo courtesy of the Lisa Law Production Archives.*

hoped might be a new human perfection. In the end we did not change very much in political realms. We did not eliminate war, racism, capitalism, exploitation, imperialism, gerrymandering, campaign finance corruption, or dependence on oil. They still exist and seem to be doing just fine. We did, however, bring them into spotlit public view on a large scale and they have become part of the political dialogue. We did do our best to refute and change them, and we made small gains.

The realm where my generation really moved the needle, however, is culture. We did this by altering the manner and concerns by which our fellow citizens actually live. Comparing the twenty-first century with facts on-the-ground as they were during the Sixties, we can point to some impressive victories:

• There is no place in America today where women have not assumed powers and authorities once denied their mothers, including gaining legal traction for equal compensation for the same work as men and the creation of institutions to protect them from domestic violence.

• There is no place in America that does not have some active environmental movement dedicated to protecting a watershed, forest, creek, meadow, or body of land. The sophistication of the environmental movement includes the successful use of the courts to block corporate pillaging and the corporations' use of our common water, air, and soil as their no-cost septic tank.

• There is no place where some of the negative consequences of Western allopathic medicine (called The Heroic School by Andrew Carnegie) are not being checked by alternative and now accepted therapies like acupuncture, homeopathy, naturopathy, yoga, ayurvedics, meditation, and massage with beneficial results.

• There is virtually no section of the country where organic food is not readily available and where local restaurants and markets have not been positively affected by Back to the Land, slow-food, and local food and wine movements.

• Similarly, in a country once dominated by Christianity—when I was a child constructing Christmas ornaments in school, no mention was ever made of Jewish holidays, for instance—alternative spiritual practices now abound, and practitioners can easily find instruction and companionship in Tibetan, Zen, Korean, Vietnamese or Vipassana Buddhism, Yoga, Wicca, Kabala, and other spiritual practices, like Bahai and Jainism.

Culture is the realm in which people actually live the life of the body. These roots sink far more deeply and cling more tenaciously to the subsoil than political ideas. Changes to enshrine these cultural beliefs and practices into political policy will take a much longer time than we realized in our twenties, but the changes outlined above are currently challenging the hegemonic models of coal and oil, of industrial farming, and of bigger-is-better and more-is-better much more successfully than the counter-culture was ever able to.

These changes are decentralizing culture in healthy ways. The concierges of the corporate/financial sector who pretend to lead us from Washington are being exposed as the shameless hirelings they have become. This cultural shift is leading toward the growth of strong regional cultural movements that are surprising in their vitality. I travel widely and often, usually crossing social boundaries. There is nowhere I've been in the last fifteen years that didn't have some hip coffeehouse(s) and gathering places, community centers, bookstores, ambitious young farmers and students coalescing into something that might grow into a deeply rooted culture. It may not look like much at the moment, that thousands of young white people, for example, are showing up and being gassed and beaten in Black Lives Matter rallies, but we can take solace in the shared values and growing commonality. As I write, for the first time in thirty-five years, a uniformed police officer has been charged with first-degree murder for shooting an adolescent sixteen times who was walking away from him. At least twelve of those shots occurred when he was lying on the ground. Before cell phones and social media, the officer's plaint that he feared for his life would have won the day. Today myriad witnesses call that what it is: bullshit. Were the police to be instructed to maintain the health and safety of the citizens before "order," civilians would not be shot so indiscriminately. The fact that they have not received such instructions is a dog-whistle signal to white people who fear African Americans, and the signal says quite clearly, "We won't let them get you." That communication rendered via silence is being challenged again (as it was during the first days of the civil rights movement) in the name of a larger and growing common cause among greater numbers of people.

And those of us who gambled everything playing for keeps in the counterculture? Whether we were right or wrong in our analysis and our tactics, we can take some pride in knowing that we were on the right side of the great divide that separates wisdom from ignorance. Our children are rightfully proud of our successes and see our failures with compassion. I can look any man or woman in the eye without flinching in shame or embarrassment. I am still proud to be part of an army that may appear disbanded but now operates behind the lines, invisibly and persistently, still seeking to secure and protect the ancient truths residing in what our poet Gary Snyder once referred to as "The Great Underground"—the great and ceaseless river of shamans, yogis, healers, artists, poets, of long-haired, nature-worshipping priestesses, seers, of dancers, craftspeople, and musicians, once again rising, bringing with its surfacing the people who know what to do with desire.

4

Keeping the Beat in the Counterculture

JACK LOEFFLER

IN THE 1950S, AS PETER COYOTE HAS ELOQUENTLY EXPLAINED, the American way was all about consumerism. Life was good if you consumed a lot of stuff, and advertisers urged you to consume more and more and more stuff.

In the United States, a small, defiant group of writers, artists, and musicians was quietly undermining the prevailing consumerist culture. It came to be known as the Beat Generation, and one of its celebrated members was poet Philip Whalen, whom I first met in North Beach and who later became my neighbor in Santa Fe. When I interviewed Philip in 1984, he addressed the genesis of the Beat Generation.

Well, Beat Generation—at this point we have to get very careful and historically accurate and whatnot and repeat what's in all the textbooks, which is true, that that name was invented by Kerouac to deal with a period in New York after the war, say, 1947. John Clellon Holmes, a friend of Jack's who has written several novels, had an assignment to write an article for the *New York Times Book Review*, or some other New York paper, about current American novel writing. So here was this new generation.

They used to say there was a Lost Generation after the First World War. What could we call where we were at after the Second World War? Jack said, "Well, why don't you call it the Beat Generation, because we're all beat. We're all tired of the war and we don't have any money. Nobody knows who we are. We're just sort of out of everything and we're kind of way out on a fringe somewhere and kind of moping along. So why don't you say Beat Generation?" So that's where that came from. It dealt, to some degree, with life around the drug scene and high "mopery" scene around Times Square in 1947, which involved Burroughs and Corso and Ginsberg and Kerouac and a number of other people. Sheri Martinelli, the painter, was around the edges there somewhere. Various other people who were later celebrated were in and around that trip.

Philip Whalen, 1984.
Photo by Jack Loeffler.

I guess it was 1954 that Ginsberg came out to San Francisco and hung around and got a job as a market researcher. He was running around in a business suit and a necktie and a white shirt, doing whatever market researchers do. At one point he went to see Kenneth Rexroth and said, in his usual way, "What's happening around here?" And Rexroth said, "Well, nothing's happening to speak of." And he said, "Why don't you make something happen? Why don't you do something yourself?" And Allen said, "Well, what'll I do?" And Rexroth said, "Hire a hall, and get your friends together and have a poetry reading." So Allen thought, "Well, that's a funny and marvelous idea. Who should I get hold of?" And Rexroth said, "Well, Philip Lamantia is in town, and in Berkeley there's a funny youngster called Gary Snyder who knows people, and Mike McClure is a young guy who is around here. You ought to find him." So Allen said, "Oh, great."

Snyder says that one day this gentleman with a business suit and a necktie and a white shirt showed up at this little shack he was living in at Berkeley and introduced himself and said, "Here I am. I'm Allen Ginsberg. Rexroth told me to come and see you and talk about doing a poetry reading." So Gary said, "Oh, okay."

I was working on the Sourdough Mountain Lookout in Washington State at that time, and Gary wrote and said to me, "As soon as you get down, you must come to Berkeley and get situated, and then we're going to have this poetry reading in October in San Francisco. This guy Allen Ginsberg has organized this funny thing and we want you to be in it." So I wrote back, "Okay, I'll see you when I get there." But the fire season ran until the middle of September that year. Anyway, I got to California before October started, and presently this big poetry bash happened on October 7, 1955.

Now then, books disagree about this, but there are various letters and other things around whereby it can easily be proved that this was done in 1955, because Ginsberg, in the summer of '55, or in the fall of '55 when I first met him, was busy cutting and polishing the version of *Howl* that he read that evening, and having a lot of fun doing it. So this reading was an unexpected excitement. Suddenly there were maybe 250 people in a very small space who had heard about it some way or another. I had helped Allen address a whole bunch of postcards announcing the thing. Then we sent it out to the mailing list that belonged to the Six Gallery, where we read. All these people showed up and were very excited about what was happening, that something was going on new and exciting. Of course, this was the first time anyone heard the *Howl* poem, and that just knocked everybody cuckoo. I think Ferlinghetti was present, and at that moment he waltzed up to Ginsberg and said, "I want to publish that thing. Give it to me."

The next thing that happened, of course, was that Rexroth was very happy and he went to Ruth Witt-Diamant, who was running the poetry center at San Francisco State, and said, "Listen, you ought to get these guys to read on your program, because they're all doing funny things that are new and exciting, and so forth." Of course, at that time her program was very, very straight. She was producing Dylan Thomas and Wystan Auden. All of the great American academic poets were coming on her series at the college, and it was always very fancy and very elegant and marvelous and expensive.

Well, anyway, she took him up on it. She simply invited all of us to come on different weeks and read at the Telegraph Hill Neighborhood Center under the sponsorship of the Poetry Center. They advertised it and whatnot, and these evenings were very successful. McClure read and Ginsberg read and Gary read and I read and I forget who all else, but in any case, those were the first public trips that we made.

The Beat literary scene in San Francisco was soon publicized in both *Look* and *Life* magazines, and North Beach became recognized as the Beat heartland on the West

Coast. Gary Snyder was one of the featured poets who read at the Six Gallery in October 1955 and became a godfather of the yet-to-be-named counterculture movement. Today, he is recognized as one of America's greatest poets and environmental philosophers.

Gary Snyder and I have worked together on a number of projects, beginning in the early 1970s. I've recorded him on numerous occasions. The following is excerpted from different conversations over many years.

GARY SNYDER: My work is not considered classical Beat generation. I'm considered a friend of them and participant in the era activities and friendships, and so forth, but in literary terms what you might call Beat literature with its emphasis on spontaneity and—you think about Jack and Allen's writings, different as they are, or Gregory Corso's writing, which is often really quite wonderful, and then Diane Di Prima's really clearly political alternative radical revolutionary outgoing statements, and so forth—I'm in another direction partly, but definitely a direction of alternatives. Alternatives in the sense of my subject matter coming so much out of the American West and the natural world, is new. And western landscapes, it's new. With the experience of reading Chinese poetry in Chinese, after 1953 I began to write more of my own poetry. Also, after two summers on lookouts, '53 and '54, in the north Cascades, I started writing *Myths and Texts*.

And so my first two books, *Riprap* and *Myths and Texts*, were basically done, basically finished, but not published by the time I left the United States in May of 1956. In the fall of '55 I was in my second or third year of studying Chinese and Japanese in Berkeley, living very, very simply in a tiny cabin, where I sat on the floor. Still visiting Kenneth Rexroth from time to time and actually doing some chores for him, like getting books out of the East Asian library for him. And then Allen Ginsberg turned up at my door. Rexroth had recommended for him to look me up. I got to know Allen quite swiftly, and then Jack Kerouac came to town and Allen said, "Jack is coming. I want you to meet him." And we did that. And Phil Whalen came back down from the Northwest, and again we all got together and introduced each other to each other. And then Allen started writing the text that would become *Howl*. And even then he also said, "Well, since none of us can seem to get published, why don't we give a poetry reading?" And that was the beginning of the plan to have the Six Gallery reading, which we did go ahead and do, later in the fall of '55.

And I had already laid my plans to go to Japan by then. And gotten my passport, gotten my boat ticket. And hung out with those guys while finishing up my course work at Berkeley and finishing my preparations to leave the country. And left on time. That was the end of that era for me.

JACK LOEFFLER: When did you first become interested in Zen Buddhism?

GS: Well, I hit that pretty directly first as an undergraduate in college, as a freshman or a sophomore. I started reading up on China and Japan and I came on basic Buddhist books and I scanned through ancient Buddhism, Ceylonese and Thai and Burmese Buddhism, Tibetan Buddhism, Chinese Buddhism, and the Japanese Buddhism. Sort of got that whole picture.

Oh yeah, a really important book for me to fall into was the *Tao Teh Ching*, the Lao Tzu book. And so when I saw Lao Tzu and somewhere I picked up in an essay or something, something on Zen Buddhism, I thought, well, it had the element of Taoism involved with it, that the Chinese school of Chan or Zen felt to me like something very right and maybe right for me, and I bore that in mind. But at the same time, I was reading about and really impressed with Tibetan Buddhism and learning more and more about Native American religious practices in different parts of the West, different parts of the country as a whole. And tried some of those things myself, like having a sweat lodge. I made myself a sweat lodge and took a sweat, and so forth. And at some point along the line, I had peyote—before I ever had marijuana.

JL: Wow, that's interesting. That had to be pretty early on.

GS: Yeah. Where did that come from? There were some people who were bringing it in to North Beach in San Francisco. But I had it up in the Klamath Indian reservation. The Indians that I was working around, logging in the Warm Springs reservation in the summer of 1952 or '53, they were doing some peyote, some of those guys were. They talked a little bit about it, sort of talked around it. But I put two and two together and I realized this was what also was happening in the Southwest.

Then I picked up—I was studying anthropology then—I picked up one of the Weston LaBarre books on the peyote cult.

JL: *The Peyote Cult*. That's the name of the book.

GS: That was the name of the book and that was the book that really laid it all out, that it had been around for a while, here's where it went, and how people responded to it, and also how it seemed to uniformly, in general, work against alcoholism. The Indian people who were taking it, many were saying, "Well, I stopped drinking after that." So it seemed like it had a munificent effect. Then I read where it got approval in a court case as an American religion.

Connecting that with all of our growing understanding of ecological science, watersheds, ecosystems, biomes, I trace a lot of that thinking back to A. L. Kroeber's book *Cultural and Natural Areas of Native North America* with its really great maps, in which all of North America is divided up by what you would now call bioregional and cultural zones. And that was where the Native people lived.

When I was still at Reed, I got that out of the library and examined it and I finally got a copy of my own. And I'm the one that made Freeman House, Peter Berg, Peter Coyote, and anybody else I could grab ahold of take a look at that book and [I'd] say, "This is really what we're talking about."

Since then there's been a lot of mapping done, really sophisticated mapping, ecosystem maps of North America, that kind of thing. And now it's all in computer mapping. So it's really possible to check everything out.

I like to say that a bioregion is the scientific or technical way of talking about it. But what everybody understands is that we all live in a watershed. And watershed thinking, which is a sub-branch of bioregional thinking, is accessible, instantly accessible. It makes instant sense and is not threatening to anybody when you first start talking about it. It only gets threatening later.

So I often start with the watershed concept and leave the more complex and farther-reaching thinking till later. But then at some point, as I did in my essays, you can also say, well, you realize of course all of planet Earth is just one watershed. It is one watershed with one water cycle going on. And add to that, there's only one little spring like this in many hundreds of millions of miles, so we better take care of this little spring in this big desert.

JL: Can you describe your sense of the evolution of the counterculture movement as a whole?

GS: I never thought of it quite like that, the counterculture movement as a whole. And, of course, every person that came to it came from some particular direction, you know, like Allen Ginsberg used to go over occasionally the difference between growing up in New York and growing up in the woods north of Seattle, in terms of how it influenced the way we would see things as counterculture thinkers, and the same would have been true of Robert Duncan or Phil Whalen or anybody in any other part of the country. [There are] some specifics there.

On the West Coast, at least it's clear that there has been a long tradition of what you might call farther left or a little more liberal attitudes in politics and religion, cultural attitudes in general, than most of the United States, although not a hundred percent different either. Enclaves of special religious and cultural interests out here as well.

I think back—there must have been other little Christian groups like that, especially in Oregon, and Finnish, Swedish, German enclaves. The Finnish and Swedes were generally pretty liberal politically, especially the Finns. And my mother, who was born in Texas, moved as a twelve year old with her mother to Seattle and turned against southern prejudice and southern discrimination very early in life and in her thinking became—this is in the late nineteen-teens and early twenties—became a feminist. Went to the University of Washington. She had to drop out because of her poverty, but she was ready to go as what would be considered a modern feminist. And there were a lot of other people like that.

She said, "Oh yeah, there was a Japanese girl in my classes at the U of W in 1922 studying together with me modern literature, and her parents grew blackberries somewhere over on Bainbridge Island or something." So the counterculture is not so surprising. It's always been around to some degree. It just hasn't been the dominant culture.

And what is the dominant culture? It's the culture that provides the story of who we are through the media and through the newspapers, and so forth. So it's actually, shall we say, the moneyed classes, who can afford to put forth their own point of view and keep paying for it, dominating the radio stations and the newspapers, as it was before.

But as you know well, because you've given me some of those books on the history of the counterculture, there have always been people who for a long time wanted to go swimming naked, wanted to eat vegetables, were naively sort of nature worshippers and not necessarily interested in East Asia or something. And there have always been a few people who were interested and would have joined in with Native Americans to some extent if they could have. Of course, the Native Americans were very conservative in their own way. So that's another story too.

Gary Snyder, 1989.
Photo by Jack Loeffler.

So it's only from one perspective, and that is like a Western American perspective of the combination of enlightenment, skepticism and atheism, political antiracism, cultural antiracism, and then a touch or paganism and nature and a touch of Native American tradition and a touch of the European political left, and all of those went toward making a particular stance. And drawing on Thoreau and Emerson in the process. Making a stance that we all felt strong in. And I'll tell you what it was in part, when I think back about it, because I remember I've said this before. It came into existence in part to resist doctrinaire Marxist Communist Party politics. Some of my friends joined the Party. Some of my friends became doctrinaire Marxists. I did not. I was tempted when I was around nineteen or twenty, but I didn't go for it for long because when I talked to them about art, about nature, and about the spiritual world, I lost them. And it was totally dismissive and didn't connect. And so I said, well, whatever they are doing that I politically sympathize with, there are some deeper things that are very important to me that they can't do and won't do, and so I'm not tempted that direction much at all. And that's the beginning of the counterculture.

The beginning of the counterculture is discovering another path, another choice away from capitalism other than European Marxist Communist ideas, Enlightenment ideas.

JL: It's selecting something that's more self-directed rather than doctrinaire.

GS: And it's more artistic and it's more psychological. It allows for the mind and it allows for art. It allows for the imagination.

5

Flashing on the Counterculture

LISA LAW

CALIFORNIA HAD ALWAYS BEEN MY HOME. Born in Hollywood in 1943, I was raised by a liberal family: my mother an attorney and my father a union organizer in the garment industry, his two brothers as well. We had money, I could tell, living in Burbank in a ranch-style home in the suburbs of LA and having a swimming pool. In my teens I got my first horse and was always riding after school in Griffith Park or down at Pollywog Pond, where the air-conditioning water came out of a pipe at the Disney Studios and created a large pond before it headed for the LA River. Those were magical days, communing with nature and being able to ride with friends.

At fifteen I moved to San Francisco to live with my mother's sister, Elaine Mikels, in Conard House, a halfway house for mental patients. It was on top of Fillmore, just before you go down the hill to the marina. It was a wonderful cream-colored Victorian house with a small garden in the back. I became president of the San Francisco Youth Hostel for a while, and we would house people from all over the world in our basement rooms. I finished high school at Galileo and then applied for school at the College of Marin, where I studied photography and music.

My father was a 16 mm man and he gave me my first camera, a Brownie. My second camera, a Honeywell Pentax, was given to me by Frank Werber, who was the manager of the Kingston Trio. He made me his personal manager, which included everything a wife would have done for him, plus. On a fateful day in 1965 we went to a Peter, Paul & Mary concert in the East Bay, and as usual, I documented the concert and then was led backstage with Frank to visit the band. That is when I got sight of my husband-to-be, Tom Law, who was the road manager for PP&M. The rest is history.

We lived together in LA, Mexico, and then in 1967 we moved back to the Bay Area. We had a little cabin in Forest Knolls that had hardly any amenities, just a table, some chairs, a couch, and a bed, but it was in a beautiful location in the trees with a little creek down the hill just below the Thelins' house.

Ron and Jay Thelin ran the Psychedelic Shop in the Haight-Ashbury district of San Francisco, where the hippie movement was taking place. We had already been introduced to pot, mushrooms, and LSD, so we weren't babes in the woods, but at

Left: *Lisa Law in Huautla de Jimenez, Oaxaca, Mexico, 1977. Photo by Cesar Estrada, courtesy of Lisa Law.* Right: *Lisa Law, 2016. Photo by Meredith Davidson.*

the same time we weren't abusers. We were right in the middle of the anti–Vietnam War movement and became very political, going to meetings, marches, and demonstrations, helping out the Diggers, and writing and photographing for the *Oracle* newspaper. Swami Bhaktivedanta-Prabhupada arrived from India and soon people were wearing orange robes and dancing in the street chanting "Hare Krishna, Hare Krishna, Krishna Krishna, Hare Hare . . ." The spiritual revolution was in full tilt and that went right along with the psychedelic revolution. You were bound to see God one way or another.

Now pregnant, I bought *The Indian Tipi* book and rented an industrial sewing machine, bought some really good army waterproof canvas and made my first Sioux tipi from scratch. I had learned sewing in home economics at John Burroughs High School in Burbank, and it was coming in handy. We set the tipi up in Nicasio outside a friend's house, and after a few times putting it up and taking it down, we figured out how to store it on top of our yellow VW bus. Now it was our home, wherever we wanted to land. We used it at the Fantasy Fair on Mount Tamalpais and then again at the Monterey Pop Festival as the trip tent: if people had taken too much acid, they could hang out with us in the tipi and center themselves. It worked very well, and it became our trademark.

On January 14, 1967, Tom and I went to the Gathering of the Tribes for a Human Be-In at Golden Gate Park with thirty thousand other people. Poets, rock groups, and political activists performed. The occasion was a new California law banning the use of the psychedelic drug LSD that had come into effect on October 6, 1966. Michael Bowen, the main organizer, invited all the speakers at the rally. They included Timothy Leary in his first San Francisco appearance, who set the tone that afternoon with his famous phrase "Turn on, tune in, drop out," and Richard Alpert (soon to be known as Ram Dass), and poets like Allen Ginsberg, who chanted mantras, Gary Snyder, and Michael McClure. Other counterculture gurus included Lenore Kandel, Lawrence Ferlinghetti, and Jerry Rubin.

What we heard from Tim Leary resonated in our minds and we decided to make the big move. We first stopped in Pyramid Lake, Nevada, to visit some new friends, Robin and David Melville, who let us set up camp at their humble digs in the desert, and that is when Robin confided to me that the only place in the United States at that point, that she knew of, to have natural childbirth was in Santa Fe, New Mexico. She had given birth to her oldest child there some five years before. I took a photo of her at that point, nursing her baby on the front porch, which I consider my Dorothea Lange photo, similar to the one she took of the mother and children in the Dust Bowl days.

Gary Snyder, Michael McClure, Allen Ginsberg, Maretta Greer, and Lenore Kandel performing at the Human Be-In, January 14, 1967. Photo courtesy of the Lisa Law Production Archives.

Robin Melville, her baby, and her daughter Nava, Pyramid Lake, Nevada, 1967.
Photo courtesy of the Lisa Law Production Archives.

After the Monterey Pop Festival, we traveled in a caravan slowly across the mountains and desert with others wanting the same changes we were after. Each time we stopped for the night, Tom would erect the tipi and we would set up our futons and blankets and I would cook over an open fire. Now I was seven months pregnant and loving every moment on the road with the tribe.

The evening that we entered New Mexico was magical. I could feel the vibrations of all the Indian tribes that lived there. It resonated under my feet, and I knew I was home.

We arrived in Santa Fe in August of 1967 and went directly to New Buffalo, a commune that was starting up in Arroyo Hondo north of Taos. Everyone was living in tipis on the barren land, so we fit right in. Tom got to work placing the newly made adobe bricks on the first walls of the main house, and I helped out in the kitchen, as well as documenting the lives of the people who were sharing the vision of Rick Klein, who had used his meager inheritance to purchase the land. They all came together to create a new utopia, planting and harvesting food and pooling their resources. Living together in the big house and in tipis only lasted one year before most of the people moved into their own homes. I think it was too rough on them, living out in the open like that. Different groups had a try at it for years and finally it became a B&B.

"While we are no longer a commune," says Bob Fies, the current owner, "New Buffalo remains a loose community of individuals connected by a common sense of ideals and a strong sense of place. As a community, we are dedicated to sustainable liv-

New Buffalo kitchen area during construction of the main house. Arroyo Hondo, New Mexico, 1967.
Photo courtesy of the Lisa Law Production Archives.

ing, a humble, open-minded outlook on the universe, and positive social change. With our neighbors and friends, we work to make the world around us a better place to be."

In front of a laundromat on Paseo del Pueblo Norte in Taos, we found a '46 Chevy flatbed that had been converted into a mobile home by a local artist. He had no more use for it, and it was for sale for only $150, which Tom paid right on the spot. What a wonderful find! Now we could move around with all we needed, and the tipi and poles fit on the plywood platform on top of the bus. We went to work beefing it up and covering the inside walls and ceiling with Indian madras.

On September 14, 1967, while visiting Barry McGuire and his family and friends in Seton Village outside of Santa Fe, we decided to go home to our tipi, which was set up on a friend's piece of land on Cerro Gordo, to fix dinner. Right in the middle of preparing a pot of rice, my water bag broke, and after dinner I started having contractions. When they were five minutes apart, Tom drove me to the Catholic Maternity Center for Natural Childbirth on Palace and Delgado Avenue. At 7:32 the next morning I gave birth to Dhana Pilar Law, our first of four children. Wow, what a trip! Tom had fallen asleep in the VW bus and they barely woke him up in time for the delivery. I stayed there for three days, learning the ropes of caring for our new addition. My friends dropped by to congratulate me and to check out little Peeps. The institute gave the mothers prenatal visits, birthing, three days live-in and postnatal, all for $200. I went on the radio to try to raise awareness of what they offered there, but they had to close because of lack of funds. You can't get that kind of service any more for that price. Even though they were a natural birth center, I swore that I was going to deliver all the rest of my children with my husband as the midwife. After all, we had the hang of it, I thought.

The Blue Bus, as we called it, became our home as we traveled around the state with Wavy Gravy and the Hog Farm Commune putting on concerts and summer solstice celebrations. We also made it to LA twice and to New York for the opening of the musical *Hair*, which Michael Butler, a friend, produced.

The Hog Farm bought some property in Llano, near Taos, and settled down there to grow some food and take a bit of a rest from their travels. We moved as a group, the Jook Savages, from farm to ranch to farm until we found some land for sale in Truchas and we all bought some parcels to start our farms. Soon after we moved into our adobe house in Truchas, I gave birth to our first son, Solar, using herbal teas picked from our own fields to help the delivery. I breastfed him for sixteen months.

We were excited to be able to work the land and plant and grow organic food. Up until that time, we had not been able to stay in one place long enough to grow our veggies, plant fruit trees, and raise animals. The older Spaniards in Truchas welcomed us with open arms because we were part of the Back to the Land movement; their own children were moving to Los Alamos and Albuquerque to work and were abandoning their parents' lifestyle. So when they saw us struggling to grow gardens and raise animals, they did everything to help us. Cipriano López taught us how to plant wheat and harvest it, as I was baking all my own bread (I even learned how to make water bagels). He also showed us how to grow and irrigate alfalfa that we used to feed our horses and goats. The mayordomo assigned everyone a day to irrigate, and we opened up our water gates and moved the water around; sometimes we were up at midnight doing it with shovels and bare feet.

We eventually had a small herd of Nubian goats and made our own cheese and yogurt and drank the milk, which was very delicious. Goat's milk is actually better for you than cow's milk because it has less protein. The kids loved it.

We planted a quarter-acre of land and grew all our own vegetables—potatoes, peas, beans, lettuce, radishes, onions, beets, and corn, even Dutch cabbage and leeks. I loved every second of growing our own food. The kids were great at shelling the peas. We bought a freezer, and I would make soups to freeze. In the fall we picked as much fruit as we could find, and I canned apples, peaches, and apricots and dried them, too, along with the mint we were growing by our pond. Prince, a huge black horse, was given to us by Pablin Montoya, who sold us the house, and every minute I had free, I would ride that wonderful beast up into the mountains or even just around the field. He was marvelous and so comfortable, as he was fat from having the run of the

Summer solstice event, Aspen Meadows, 1969. Photo courtesy of the Lisa Law Production Archives.

field every day. We cut our own alfalfa, and Tom and his friend Tom Watson built a barn to keep it out of the rain and protect the goats and chickens from rough weather. Cipriano would bring over his bailer to bail the hay, and we would trade him some bales for doing it. I adored kidding the goats and playing with the kids. Our children did too. Farm life suited all of us, and we had such an abundance of everything that I was even able to sell baskets of food out of the back of our Citroen station wagon. I sold out every time I ventured from the house. Tom had built a greenhouse off the west side of the house, and I planted arrangements of succulents that I would take to the farmer's market on the Santa Fe Plaza on Saturdays and to Los Alamos on Sundays and sell out to the locals. Tom and his friend Parker Mead built a redwood Japanese *furo* bath that we heated with a fire and cooled off with the hose. When there was snow on the ground, we would get nice and hot and then jump out of the tub and lie flat on the snow-covered ground face down, turn over, and then jump back into the tub, where our bodies tingled from our pores opening up and closing. We would spend almost every evening in the tub with the kids and shared it with a lot of friends. It was delicious.

I found that the mountain people accepted us more than the city folk. One time I was driving around town in my hippie bus in Santa Fe and someone stoned my vehicle. Now, my bus, Silver, is honored in the Fiesta Parade each year by hundreds of families who think that we are the most colorful float in the parade.

Aerial photo of Woodstock, 1969. Photo courtesy of the Lisa Law Production Archives.

During the summer solstice celebration in 1969 in Aspen Meadows, one of the producers of the Woodstock Music & Art Fair from upstate New York asked Hugh Romney (aka Wavy Gravy) and the Hog Farm if we could help out with the production of the concert, mainly the free kitchen and security. Because we were a large group of hippies, schooled in the dos and don'ts of caring for those as high as we were, we were a much-needed commodity at the festival. So on the first week of August of 1969 they sent an American Airlines jumbo jet from New York to pick us up in Albuquerque and fly us to LaGuardia Airport. It was funny seeing them load up our tipi poles in the baggage compartment. When we arrived, a group of buses were waiting for us and so was the press, wanting to know what our role was going to be at the concert and wanting to know what we'd do for security. Wavy's immediate answer was "Lemon pies and seltzer bottles." We also helped out at the Texas Pop Festival a month later.

I believe the Woodstock Festival was one of the most important events of my life. That is why, even though there were four hundred thousand people on the grounds, over a million will tell you they were there. In actuality, many people were trying to get there, but the New York State Thruway was closed to traffic. There was nowhere to park your car, and when you did park it, you had to walk miles and miles to get to the concert grounds. The Hog Farm and friends arrived two weeks early, and I volunteered to drive into town in a big truck with Peter Rabbit to buy supplies and utensils for the masses. The producers gave me $6,000 and I used it up in two days. Back at Yasgur's farm, I rode on a flatbed to buy out farmers' rows and rows of vegetables to cook up with the bulgur wheat I had purchased. Once the festival got under way, volunteers did all the work of preparing and serving the food, and Jahanara and I just made sure they had what they needed. We built five two-sided serving booths, and sometimes we would serve granola right next to the stage so that people didn't have to leave their places where they were listening to the music. Our daughter, Pilar, spent most of her time playing with the other Hog Farm kids, but she slept with us in our tipi at night. To her, it was like being in a huge playground.

Once back in New Mexico we carried on with our farm life. Michael Shrieve, Santana's drummer, came to live with us to recuperate from his life on the road. It was a good respite for him, which he reminds me of whenever I see him.

In 1968 during one of our trips to Los Angeles, we studied yoga with Yogi Bhajan and brought him to Santa Fe in 1969 to teach the folks at the summer solstice. He also performed an Indian marriage ceremony, and Tom and I were married along with

Tom Law pitching a tipi at Woodstock, 1969. Photo courtesy of the Lisa Law Production Archives.

Yogi Bhajan. Photo courtesy of the Lisa Law Production Archives.

seven other couples. Tom started teaching yoga on a piece of land off West Alameda that Dawson Hayward volunteered, and soon after that, with help from his students, Yogi Ji built an ashram in Española that is still there today. The spiritual revolution was in full swing, and many healers, past life regressers, rebirthers, and crystal healers were sprinkled all over the state. Andrei Codrescu came through town during the filming of his documentary, *Road Scholar*, and asked me to produce the New Mexican segment about the spiritual movement. The film grossed more than any other documentary that year.

My dear friend Bonnie Watson decided to start a toy store in Truchas, and so was born the Dandelion Toy Shop. Kirsten Register Coglan spent a lot of time helping us as well, with her little babies at her side. Besides the toys, we also added to the shelves herbs, bulk grains, soy sauce kegs, honey, and herbal laxatives. A few of the locals sold their handmade items out of the store too, like matchstick crosses, crocheted hats and other clothes. We were now part of the community of Truchas, and even though the town had a tough mode, we sort of fit in. The view from the Sangre de Cristo Mountains was spectacular. When it snowed, we were blanketed in at least two feet of white powder, and we had to plow our way out of our driveway to go to town. When the snow melted, it was a mud bog unless we drove out when it was frozen. Truchas was a challenge, but it was exciting to be a part of the elements. In the spring, the mayordomo called for a day to clean out the acequias, and we all met up at the beginning of the ditch and cleaned it out together, leaving piles of mud and grass on the side. It was a good way to get to know our neighbors. The kids went to Head Start in Truchas, but for kindergarten they took a bus down the hill to Cordova.

In 1969 Dennis Hopper bought the Mabel Dodge Luhan house in Taos and set up editing *The Last Movie*, which had just filmed in Cuzco, Peru. Tom and I would go up to visit him along with a group of actors, artists, and poets to watch the screenings and give our nod to his edits. Alejandro Jodorowsky visited to put in his two cents, and I fell in love with his philosophy. One day in the Tony Lujan house, I told Alejandro he was my teacher and he commented, "There are no teachers and there are no students." I don't know if I agree with that but it sure made an impression on me. He had just directed *El Topo*, which is the most highly revered, symbolic western film to date.

Peter Fonda was back in the state, too, directing and acting in *The Hired Hand*, which he filmed in Cuba and the San Juan Pueblo, New Mexico. He and Dennis had been in the state filming *Easy Rider*, a film made for only $400,000 that changed the way Hollywood looked at filmmaking. I hung out with Peter at the Warm Springs in Cuba and gave him massages and brought smoothies to the set. Always with my camera, I got some good stills of the filming. Severn Darden, a comedian friend who lived in LA, was in the film too and eventually moved to Santa Fe in the 1990s.

Mati Klarwein took up residency in Santa Fe on Acequia Madre with his wife Caterine Milinaire, who wrote the book *Birth*, the only one of its kind at the time; it showed women the alternatives to a hospital birthing experience. She used a lot of my photos and even told stories of my births. Mati was busy in his studio painting parts of the Aleph sanctuary, as well as album covers for Malcolm X and Miles Davis. He painted the cover of *Abraxas* for Carlos Santana as well. When we visited Dennis Hopper, Mati loved to play the atomic gongs that Tony Price had made. They were hanging in a lean-to that was built right over the acequia that ran past the house.

Tony Price traveled around the North with the Jook Savages and eventually settled near Santa Fe, where he made his atomic art to ward off nuclear annihilation. He would go up to Los Alamos every Wednesday, wait till the gates opened at the Black Hole, and rush in with the others to find great pieces of metal that he turned into atomic figures and masks. I would sometimes follow him up there to capture him diving into the piles of metal, looking for the perfect pieces. We were both born on March 8, so we had an affinity for each other. He asked that I exhibit his art if I ever was able to realize a Museum of the Sixties.

Ram Dass visited the state often and helped start the Neem Karoli Ashram in Taos, which I visited regularly. Ram Dass wrote the introduction to my book in 1987, so to thank him, I photographed him every time I saw him on his visits, and my

Victor Maymudes next to the Road Hog, 1970s. Photo courtesy of the Lisa Law Production Archives.

photographs of him were used in his books and audio and video releases. He was the spiritual voice for many of us and still is today.

Allen Ginsberg, Peter Orlovsky, and Gregory Corso would come to town periodically to recite poetry at various events, and I even had them as guests at my home during their travels.

All of these folks were supporters of the American Indian Movement, as was I, and in the 1980s I was the head of the Big Mountain support group in Santa Fe, spending a lot of time on the reservation attempting to stop the relocation of the Navajos. Floyd Westerman and I became good friends. He was very involved with that movement and wrote songs and spoke on many occasions to huge groups of supporters. On one occasion, I organized a demonstration and march from the Roundhouse in Santa Fe to Sweeney Auditorium with members of AIM and Navajo leaders so that they could demonstrate how they were being wrongly treated by the government.

In 2015 El Museo Cultural de Santa Fe gave me a great space to exhibit my photographs and collections of memorabilia, including many of my photos of musicians, the Haight-Ashbury, the march against the war in Vietnam in San Francisco, the movement back to the land in New Mexico, the mountain men of the North, blotter art, and Wavy Gravy's collage pieces. Tony Price had a prominent place where I displayed moments of his life and four pieces of his sculptures.

New Mexico has been good to my ever-growing family and me. After I raised my kids in Santa Fe, I bought some land with three of my children and built a two-story pumice house that is totally off the grid, where I grew my own vegetables and fruit trees. I now live in Santa Fe, where again I have a garden and fruit trees, as well as an office that I built, where I work on my photographs and writings. I have written two books on the Sixties and directed a documentary, *Flashing on the Sixties: A Tribal Document*, and have been published in numerous books and magazines about that era. There is never a dull moment: I keep busy with my collections, licensing footage and images, my political and social activities, documenting every good cause I can and donating to many causes, and playing with my five grandchildren.

My wish is to leave traces behind. I would like to have a permanent collection of my work available for all the generations to come so that they may see what influenced us to arrive where we are today.

Peter Rowan performing. Photo courtesy of Peter Rowan.

6

Gigging High with Peter Rowan

PETER ROWAN

AS I WRITE THIS, MONDAY, JANUARY 11, 2016, the front page of the *New York Times* shows a photograph of an antigovernment activist brandishing an American flag, riding on a horse across the snowy sagebrush desert of an Oregon wildlife refuge. A party of armed right-wing militias is taking over federal lands and going to court to restore to local ranchers BLM and other federally administered lands. Never mind back to the Native Americans. And there is actor Sean Penn consorting with Mexican drug kingpin Joaquín Guzmán Loera, El Chapo, who was recaptured last week after a year on the run following his escape from a Mexican prison. Mr. Penn's interview with El Chapo was published this past Saturday in *Rolling Stone* magazine, much to the surprise and consternation of journalists and government officials. Where is the counterculture now?

It is difficult to say what is the mainstream culture of 2016 and who or what is the "counter" culture, when the Internet and smart phones are not controlled by corporate mass media. We live in a "culture" of worldwide terrorist attacks, interminable war in the Middle East, mass gun murders in our schools, on our streets. "Bring the war home!" was a Sixties rallying cry. Well, folks, the war is here. But the streets are not filled with marching protesters. Everyone is their own private counterculture spokesperson today. You can blog, you can Facebook, you can let everybody know . . . and who cares? And then comes along a movement, Occupy Wall Street, or Stamp Money out of Politics, and every citizen of the United States and people all over the world can instantly share this information. Is it Kulture, as Ezra Pound called it, or is it counterculture?

I was born in seemingly simpler times near the end of World War II. The rise of the military industrial complex and the explosion of mass-media propaganda was, in my generation's view, the Kulture to counter with our own youth revolution in the Sixties. Oh those were simpler times indeed; a photograph on the cover of *Life* magazine of Elvis Presley gyrating and wailing his rockabilly blues to pubescent shrieking baby boomers turned the youth of the United States from the conservative culture of their parents to the birth of the counterculture, music of the Devil. It was legion, and its name was Rock 'n' Roll! That explosion of youthful energy in 1957 became the countercultural youth movement of the Sixties.

Let me tell you how it was for me as a small boy born on the fourth of July in Boston, the Cradle of Revolution. Two things stand out in my early memories. I remember the blackouts at night so that enemy bombers couldn't target our lights. My parents let me squeeze the red dye in the margarine pack to make it look like butter during the war rationing.

I grew up in the quaint New England community of Wayland, off the Old Boston Post Road. It was a pretty country town, and square dancing was a fun thing to do on a Friday night. Being polite, bowing to your partner, the à-la-main, the grand right and left, and the more decorous ballroom dancing on Saturday night made a nice weekend for "good" children on the verge of adolescence. We grew up during the early days of local television. Big Brother Bob Emery was like a polite uncle when he toasted us over WGBH, "My favorite drink is milk. I hope it's yours!"

Two things always caught my attention: adult intoxication and the power of music to entrance us all, large and small.

My Uncle Jimmie came back from New Caledonia when the War of the Pacific ended. He had been trained at Camp Tarawara on the Parker Ranch in Waimea, Big Island, Hawaii. Jimmie had a crazy joy about him. He would lift his elbow, knees akimbo, raise his glass of gin and tonic, and shout, "Hubba hubba ding ding! Mean, I mean!" in a toast with the grown-ups and a wink at us kids. He came back from New Caledonia in the Pacific with grass skirts and coconut-shell bras, strumming on a Martin baritone ukulele he said that he had won at a poker game in the Hubba Hubba bar in Honolulu. I begged him to teach me how to play. I learned "Five Foot Two," "Ain't She Sweet," and the mysterious, powerful "Bye Bye Blackbird." He didn't really know all the chords to "Blackbird," but he could pull it off, naturally!

When we heard Little Richard's war cry, "A womp-bomp-a-lula, a-womp-bam-boom!" everything changed. I immediately formed a rock 'n' roll combo with my close friends. We called ourselves the Cupids and drove to gigs in drummer Chris Scott's dad's station wagon to play sock hops, where the girls wore white socks and kicked off their penny loafers to rock around the clock with those bashful boys. Curfew 8:30 p.m.!

One night on the way home from a dance, we stopped in Harvard Square, where we had heard beatniks and musicians hung out. Sure enough, there were some black dudes with serious goatees playing conga drums in a café. They were drinking strong espresso and jamming until it was time for their next set at Lennie's. "Hey, you boys wanna cop a buzz?"

And so it began, the curious journey of Purple Pango, Panama Red, the noxious weed, the late-night-third-set smoky, groovy, let-me-lay-this-on-you-cats, eye-poppin', ear-candy, have-a-hit-joint-rollin'-jam-session days and nights that became the life-style for us, the youth of America. Our parents were square, with their corny clothes, their cocktails, their haircuts, man, so square! Are you hip? We devoured Kerouac, Ginsberg, the antiwar Ernest Hemingway. Artists and musicians gave us a vision. We wandered into the fog of idealism and hedonism. We lost friends in the Vietnam War. Eye contact became our signal. One look and you knew if the stranger you had just met was cool or uncool; a look and "Whew, far out!" told you all you needed to know. It was all superficial, but the youth were communicating to each other with their new fashion and slang. We were getting far out listening to *Word Jazz* by Ken Nordine, free jazz, Ornette Coleman, John Coltrane, Miles!

The "shot heard 'round the world" was fired in Concord, Massachusetts, about seventeen miles north of my hometown of Wayland. The first battle of the American Revolution took place at the North Bridge spanning the Concord River—river of peace, river of revolution, river of patriotic evolution. Seeds were planted here for many social movements—from pacifism to vigilante patriotism. Near Concord is fabled Walden Pond, where Henry David Thoreau lived in his rustic cabin. Ralph Waldo Emerson, Nathaniel Hawthorne, and the Alcott family lived in Concord, where Emerson once asked Thoreau, who was behind bars in the local jail, "Henry David, whatever are you doing in there?" to which Thoreau answered, "Ralph Waldo, whatever are you doing out there?" Or so the story goes. The New England Transcendentalists certainly helped open the doors of American intellectual life to the influence of Buddhist and Vedic ideas then entering the young country's literary and spiritual life. Modern poets from Frost to Kerouac continued that New England simplicity until the Beats began to be not beaten down, but beatific. We inherited that transcendent idealism in the 1960s.

We were reading Aldous Huxley's *The Doors of Perception* and *Brave New World*, Thoreau on civil disobedience, *Lord of the Flies*. We saw through new eyes what US imperialist invasions of foreign nations had done: genocide of native peoples of America, suppression of Hawaii, invasion of Vietnam, toppling elected governments in South America. The hedonism of the American youth was played out to a lurid backdrop of the deadly televised war in Vietnam. Music and marijuana had universal appeal. I wanted to "take it to the streets" and speak out with my generation, but it seemed I always had a gig to do. To play music for people, all people, whether in some country bar or honky-tonk, to sailors and whores dancing at the Hillbilly Ranch in Boston's Combat Zone. Or to the growing college-aged audience for blues and bluegrass, roots music from the old American South little changed since the end of the War of the Confederacy a century before. It seemed the ghosts of history were rising up for one last big show across the nation as the Apocalypse began to rage. We threw the *I Ching* coins—they read *Thunder on the Mountain*, an exposé of the coal industry.

Living in the South in the Sixties, being Bill Monroe's guitarist and a Bluegrass Boy allowed me to see another, hidden side of American life. I wasn't a southerner by birth, but I was raised by my parents to respect everyone, to be polite. I never expected that their upbringing of me would be its own reward. Segregation was rampant; all over the South were "colored only" drinking fountains, "colored only" restrooms. I hadn't joined the political movement against social injustice in America, but I had migrated into the heartland of segregation. Beyond the keeping of safe distances and the "separate but equal" social status quo, something more powerful in the socially complicated southern society was revealed: black music. Otis Redding had soul-shouted to the white youth at the Monterey Pop Festival. He told them, he told the nation, "That's how strong my love is." And we heard him, we believed him, and it opened our hearts, and for a moment in history we had the vision beyond politics. The Staple Singers, Odetta, Otis, James Brown, Jimi Hendrix: the soul of white America was beginning to feel its possibilities. Its sacred responsibilities.

Bill Monroe's music, too, was born from the old South. Fiddle tunes from his Uncle Penn Vandiver, country blues from Penn's black sidekick guitarist, Arnold Shultz from New Orleans. Monroe himself acknowledged that New Orleans was home base to the Bluegrass Boys when he formed his own band and toured Louisiana, Texas, far beyond the Appalachian Mountains of the Southeast.

"Oh man, you could hear any kind of music there, back then. You had the sock-time, jump-time, the stomp, and you had the slow-drag." Monroe translated every sound he heard into his own musical history of country rags and hollers, hoedowns, gospel and fiddle tunes. "Pete, I've kept as much out of bluegrass as I have put into it!"

It was in Harvard Square, in a record store where they let you listen to vinyl records, that I first heard Bill Monroe's version of Leadbelly's "Black Girl" sung as "In the Pines." That authenticated bluegrass for me. I could sing the blues in bluegrass music; I could find my voice there. There was no segregation in the soul of music. Music crossed the racial divide, slipping past the guardians of exclusivity, inviting all to follow. Bob Dylan captured that invitation in "Mr. Tambourine Man": "In the jingle jangle morning I'll come following you."

My very first show as a Bluegrass Boy was with Doc Watson and Bill Monroe at Boston's Symphony Hall. It was Doc's birthday, and the double bill was organized by folklorist Ralph Rinzler. After a blazing duet set with Doc and Bill, a hair-raising set by Doc solo, we took the stage with Bill Monroe. The banjoist genius Bill Keith, Tex Logan on fiddle with Gene Lowenger, Everette-Allen Lilly on bass—we were inspired! After the show Bill said to me, "Peter, you ought to come to Nashville. I can he'p you!" So I became a Bluegrass Boy in the tradition. I worked with Bill from 1964 through early 1967. I once heard a reporter ask Mr. Monroe if he didn't think that Elvis Presley had ruined his famous song "Blue Moon of Kentucky" by making it a rock and roll hit. "Nossir," said Bill, straight-faced, "them'uns were powerful checks."

My time spent with my mentor, singer-mandolinist Joe Val learning all the old Louvin Brothers and Blue Sky Boys vocal duets on long summer evenings in

Wayland had taught me the details of two-part harmonies, the backbone of blue-grass duet singing. Joe was the living history of old-time country and bluegrass in the Boston area. He was there at the Hillbilly Ranch in Park Square when fiddler Tex Logan introduced the Lilly Brothers and banjo powerhouse Don Stover to the mostly southern sailors and soldiers disembarked at the Boston Naval Yard from the European campaigns of World War II. Tex Logan told me that one night someone in the audience had made off with Bea Lilly's Confederate hat during the band's break during the radio show on a Sunday at the Park Hotel near Boston Commons. Older brother Everette saw it all go down, and the next weekend when the Confederate Mountaineers took to the stage at the Park Hotel, there was the Yankee thief wearing Brother Bea's Confederate mountaineer hat. And while they were on the air, Everette walked off stage up to the thief, laid a .45 caliber pistol on the front-row table, and said in his most pleasant West Virginia manner, "Look-a-here, dear buddy, I do believe you are a-wearin' my brother Bea's hat!" The man got up and very graciously handed Bea his hat.

Only five years after leaving Nashville and the world of Bill Monroe and the Bluegrass Boys, I found myself again on the shores of the Left Coast, the golden rolling hills of California. The air was full of promise, the tang of eucalyptus and of a wilder weed!

Since leaving the Bluegrass Boys, I had reunited with David Grisman and formed a band we called Earth Opera. Originally David and I, coming from acoustic bluegrass, were a duet of mandocello and guitar, with me singing my original songs. We signed with Elektra records and president Jac Holzman sent us over to Mort Lewis, the manager of Simon and Garfunkel.

Mort asked us to agree to have New York musicians orchestrate the twelve-song demo we had done, produced by David's friend Peter Segal. Were they asking us to allow them to transform our acoustic purity into rock 'n' roll? It was a formula that worked for Paul and Arty, so why not for us? But David and I were "band" guys, and anyway, weren't the Beatles a band? We felt we were being asked to prostitute our music. Besides, we had a group of hungry musicians waiting for us in a flooded basement in Cambridge! We weren't about to let them languish, splashing around on floating planks, while we made hit records in New York that we didn't even play on. Oh no, using our demo as the basic tracks for a commercial record recorded over our pure acoustic music? No way.

The band, Earth Opera, did break some new ground. There were a lot of jazz saxophone players in Boston and New York who had learned bebop after Bird, Coltrane, and Miles, but times had changed and there was less and less of an audience for pure bop. The jazz horn players loved to jam, and two saxophones could follow improvised guitar chords like a swarm of bees! Grisman and I took up the saxophone.

We spent many a stoned and happy day out in the fields of Wayland tootling away on our horns. We were experiencing what jazz bass-clarinetist Eric Dolphy had said: "Man, music is EVERYWHERE!" And so were we!

Earth Opera recorded a free jazz intro to my song "The Great American Eagle Tragedy," which became a sort of anthem for war resisters, draft dodgers, AWOL recruits seeking sanctuary in church basements around Boston. No, this was definitely not the Grand Ol' Opry anymore! We were playing for our contemporaries and had become a sort of sideshow in the official counterculture movement! So while race riots and protest marches filled the streets of America, we blew our horns and turned up the volume on our amps. We toured, opening for fellow Elektra artists Jim Morrison and the Doors. A theatrical commedia-del-art-style show evolved for Earth Opera. Bombastic and energized, we lunged like Beckett characters onward through the fog! Were we following our vision? Well, truly it was chaos and anarchy, but most likely true to the zeitgeist of our times.

I remember on tour in Florida, long-haired, bearded fans hanging out. One scraggly dude pointed to the far-off sparkling waves off the Florida Keys, "Man, you know, Lemuria is out there, under the ocean, man! Yeah, a friend of mine was out there the other day, skin diving, man, and you know what? He saw the columns of old Atlantis, man, Lemur just under the waves, on the bottom, you know? Far out!"

That night David and I were offered some very strong weed before the show. The rest of the band was nervous because we could easily lose our way in a song and completely blow the arrangement, "free space" we euphemistically called those moments. A short, hairy dude hands me a fat joint. "Here, man, try this." He laughed in a fit of coughing. "Whew, man, far out!" I shook my head. "Ah, no, like really, man, I'll lose my way . . . the band won't follow." "Yeah, man, but that's what I'm talking about, yesssss! It's such a trip to watch you recover, man!"

Earth Opera dissolved on the road on a West Coast tour. The brotherhood of bonding reached a breaking point when we played Cleveland. Race riots were burning the town down. A loose guitar string on my electric kept touching the back of the neck of our saxophonist while he was at the microphone singing. Every time the string touched his neck, he screamed. And I thought, man, far out! He's really into it!

I decided to go back to Nashville from Boston. My lady and I drove down in a Volkswagen bug, with two dogs, my guitar, and two suitcases in the tiny back seat. We were happily visiting with friends and hanging out in the studios when I got a call from ex–Bluegrass Boy fiddler Richard Greene. He was in a rock 'n' roll band called Seatrain, and did I want to come out west and join? So we drove on out and spent two years being produced by George Martin both in London and Marblehead, Massachusetts. It was a very disciplined band, and I learned that if you can get the first four bars of a song right, the rest is a groove. Same as it had been with Bill Monroe, but Bill never counted in the song! You just had to know the time. With Seatrain we focused so intently that we could get the first two notes perfectly in time, and the rest was just a piece of cake!

Seatrain moved to the East Coast for work, college concerts, opportunities. I was still grateful for rent and phone money, but the incessant touring was wearing me out. And I longed to play bluegrass again.

David Grisman had moved to Stinson Beach in Marin County, California, and was producing a record of my two brothers, Chris and Lorin. I missed singing with my brothers, and playing with David as well. I thought the "free space" was out there on the Left Coast still. In Utah we camped up on Muley Point overlooking the San Juan River in the canyon below. In a thunderstorm I stood on the mesa precipice and let the deities of the elements wash over me, wash me clean of the strict-tempo strictures, open my heart to the mystic Southwest! The next morning I began to write a long poem that developed into a new song, "In the Land of the Navajo." With my cheeks full of peyote and ginseng, the song told me its story as we drove along. I added some native-style chanting at the end and wondered who would want to play this song.

We moved into an old barn in Stinson Beach where Gregg Irons and other artists were putting together Slow Death counterculture horror comics. Like R. Crumb's, Gregg's acerbic vision was part of the San Francisco alternate universe of the time. Grisman and I would meet out on the sand dunes in the morning in a cloud of smoke to pick bluegrass. We were twenty-five, and this was barefoot childhood's last dream. One morning Dave said, "Hey, man, you know, García lives just up the hill. He loves to pick." "OK, let's go!"

Jerry's generous spirit had led him to champion my brothers' music. He was like a giant heart that beat for the goodness he found in people. "Far out!" and a beatific grin were his response. Negative vibes were simply a laugh and "Bummer." He met us at his front gate with his banjo and was picking away! With bassist John Kahn and Florida fiddling wizard Vassar Clemens, we were a band with no name. One day at rehearsal, wondering about a group name, there was a pause; through the smoke Jerry spoke, "We're, like, 'Old and in the Way,'"

We finally made it up to Ken Kesey's farm in Oregon. After an evening of home-cooked food and some lazy hours by the campfire, we listened to Kesey hold forth and mostly smile. The next night was show time with Asleep at the Wheel opening. Garcia encouraged everything musical, and the chanting at the end of "Land of the Navajo" now had moments where "free space" really opened up. As we entered the dressing room after our set, which had been plagued with technical sound problems, the usual mumbled grumblings started. Jerry filled the dressing room with his eyes blazing. "No thoughts!" he glared. "No thoughts!"

THE FREE MEXICAN AIRFORCE

In the Morellos Mountains
cabacinos are planting their fields
Where the ghost of Zapata rides a horse
that can still outrun the wind
There free in the sky and clear out of sight
It's the Free Mexican Airforce, flying tonight

In the city of angels
a cowboy is cooling his heels
Remembering that god gave us herbs
and the fruits of the fields
but a criminal love that makes outlaws
of those who seek light
paid the Free Mexican Airforce,
Mescalito riding his white horse
yeah the Free Mexican Airforce is flying tonight

flying so high

how strange that an innocent herb
causes money to burn
the day will kill you for making
those rich fat cats squirm
but the fools who make rules
with no difference between wrong or right
that's why the Free Mexican Airforce is flying tonight...

Uncle Sam it is a misery
but a nix on the fields of Carrero
Saying shoot down all gringos and wetbacks
that dare wear sombreros
Either run for the hills, surrender
or stand up and fight
Or join the Free Mexican Airforce,
Mescalito riding his white horse
the Free Mexican Airforce, flying tonight

they're flying so high

(instrumental)

Is that marijuana destroying the minds of the young?
The confusion continued for power and greed in all form
May the borders of evil fall to the smugglers of light
Where the Free Mexican Airforce is flying tonight

In San Antonio they tell me
that power and money are one
They can buy us or sell you
to keep you afraid on the run
But no one can stop us,
my vision is nearly in sight
and the Free Mexican Airforce,
Mescalito riding his white horse
the Free Mexican Airforce is flying tonight

flying so high...

Some are smoking *colitas*
while others are loading their guns
blowing smoke from their six-shooters
spinning their barrels for fun
contrabandistas, banditos alike
were the Free Mexican Airforce who were flying tonight

High in the hills we are harvesting sweet sensimilla
The law wants it all cos they know
that the wild weed can free ya
And freedom for us is the prison
for the rulers of might
That's why the Free Mexican Airforce is flying tonight
The Free Mexican Airforce,
Mescalito riding his white horse

The Free Mexican Airforce is flying tonight!

Siddiq Hans von Briesen, 2015. Photo by Jack Loeffler.

7

Lama Foundation and the Origin of *Be Here Now*

SIDDIQ HANS VON BRIESEN

AT THE TIME, IT SEEMED WE WERE HEADING INTO SHANGRI-LA. It was a long dirt road in northern New Mexico leading up the mountain. All around and toward the Rio Grande behind us were low clouds of mist from the rain, giving the forest and valley a magical quality.

Frances and I, with our two children, were stopping by to visit Steve and Barbara Durkee, my brother-in-law and my sister, on our way to see family in California. It was August 1967, a time of clear mornings and afternoon thunderstorms. A yellow school bus stood at the upper end of a sloping meadow, in the middle of which was the foundation of a building and a basin of scooped-out dirt where adobes were being made. Steve and Barbara had finally found the place where they could pursue their vision of a community in the Southwest, a vision that began during their days of artistic and multimedia creative work in and around New York City. They had spent two years since leaving the East, some of it with Richard Alpert, later Ram Dass, and most of it looking for land in the Southwest and sharing their vision with others.

We spent three days there while I tried to hold my own helping to make adobes with a crew of Indians from Taos Pueblo, led by Henry Gomez, the oldest. Barbara cooked out of the bus, and we slept in tents. During that visit, Barbara said, "I feel like a postgraduate hippie." Steve spoke of Herman Rednick, a meditation teacher in Taos, a painter of mystical visions, and an advisor. He had told them, "I can't help you with a utopian community because it has been tried and won't work. If you want to create a spiritual community, I can help you." His advice: have regular meals, nourish body,

Barbara Durkee (aka Asha) at Lama, 1970s. Photo by Seth Roffman.

Interior of dome at Lama. Photo by Seth Roffman.

spirit, and mind each day—and if you want to make faster progress on the spiritual path, do not use drugs. They followed this advice, including no drugs, and the number of people interested in their revised vision, instead of dozens, became just three: Steve, Barbara, and Jonathan Altman, the three founders. Herman had also discovered the land for sale and had persuaded Steve to look at it before closing on another location. I consider Herman, since deceased, to be Lama's godfather, though he was quite critical of many things that went on there, including the publication of *Be Here Now*.

Steve was indirectly influenced by the teachings of G. I. Gurdjieff, through friends well versed in those teachings, and this played a part in his formulation of the bylaws of the foundation, incorporated in the spring of 1968 as Lama Foundation (here called Lama, though the entire downhill neighborhood is called Lama). Lama has several meanings: in the old, local Spanish, it referred to a kind of mud, which must have trapped many wagons on the old road to Questa as they passed though the tiny Spanish village called Lama. In Tibetan, it means "teacher." In Aramaic, the language of Jesus, it means "Why?" Steve was as brilliant at words as anyone I have met, and this conjunction of meanings appealed to him very much.

The whole project drew us strongly. As we drove down the road at the end of three intense days, Frances asked, "Why are we leaving?" I answered the obvious, that we had family to visit—but I felt that even if we never came back, it would be a "home" for us.

In Taos, I experienced some magic. As we were getting gas, an old Indian came up to me and began conversing, mentioning a powwow in Gallup. I told him we had been up at Lama, working with Henry Gomez. He said, "He's my boy!" Then he asked for a ride. He rode with us for no more than fifty yards and asked to get out at the post office. He said, "God bless you"—and for the next hundred miles and several hours more, I felt high as a kite! We learned later that he was a Taos elder, that his grandfather had brought peyote to New Mexico and he was regarded as a holy man by many who had met him. He was Joe Gomez, Grandpa Joe, also a leader in the peyote church. There were several times in the following years when Grandpa Joe's presence on Lama's land seemed to have given rise to an unexpected blessing.

Our second visit was for three weeks in 1968, again in the late summer. There were twelve people on the land. The zonahedral framework of the main dome (designed by Steve Baer) had been completed, and the kitchen, uphill in line with the dome, was under construction. Everyone worked very hard. Wings of the dome included a commons room, a washroom, and a bathhouse on the south side and a library and a planned meditation room on the north side.

Steve told us of a visit by a group of Taos elders, led by Grandpa John, Joe's brother. Steve had led them around and described what he envisioned. At the end of the tour, John said to Steve, "You white people, you've lost your way. We Indians, we

Left: *Interior of dome at Lama. Photo courtesy of Siddiq Hans von Briesen.*

Right: *Lama, 1970s. Photo by Seth Roffman.*

haven't lost our way. But our way is not your way!" So much for calling the meditation room a kiva! It finally became the Prayer Room. Steve thought that while Grandpa Joe represented love and kindness, Grandpa John represented the law, strict and somewhat fierce. This was my experience, too.

Lama's bylaws aimed at a division of power. The trustees selected the officers, but the continuing members elected the trustees. And decisions were to be made by consensus. Steve's leadership was only slightly compromised by consensus, because of his charisma, the clarity of his vision, and his brilliance in articulating it. Barbara also led, more quietly and with more attention to individual needs. Later she said that it was important for everyone to have a door they could close. Several A-frames had been built already, and it was clear that only community functions would be shared under one roof—kitchen, dining room, bathhouse, library, prayer room, central dome.

The effort toward consensus led to very conservative governance and enabled a strong tradition to be established in a few years rather than a few decades. Consensus at its worst represented a one-person veto and at its best manifested a meeting of hearts. We experienced both. Consensus decisions included who would be allowed to stay—anyone who said no was expected to say why and might be challenged by the others. It was an interesting and important experiment in group psychology. When years later Lama suffered severe internal conflict, strict consensus was modified to "seeking a spirit of consensus." This remains an experiment in progress, even today.

In 1969, we came to stay. I had just dropped out of physics with severe existential anxiety. We had been involved in Gurdjieff work ourselves for over five years. Lama presented an opportunity to continue inner work in the context of a vision that we were drawn to. Barbara told us that in the fall, Baba Ram Dass, formerly Richard Alpert, was planning a seven-week "ashram" at Lama and we had to have his permission to stay for that. He was expected to come by for a visit, and we could ask him then.

We did. At the end of my interview with Ram Dass, he asked if I had any questions. I asked what I thought might be a heretical question: "Why go on the spiritual path?" He smiled and thought for a few moments, then said, "Because nothing else is enough." It remains the only truly rational answer I know, and for me, it remains the case. During the ashram weeks, each of us spent a week in hermitage, with Ram Dass visiting each of us. He told me that while most people there were working on opening their hearts, the fourth *chakra*, I had yet to open my third chakra, having to do with power and control. This led to some central insights through my experience at Lama during the following two years and continuing ever since.

I believe that *Be Here Now* was seeded during that ashram in conversation between Ram Dass and Steve. There was no thought of a commercially available book, but Ram Dass wanted to do a fifty-city tour and provide to those who attended something in the way of guidance that they could keep. Conceived was a "core book" based on transcripts of Ram Dass's talks, a manual for parents who needed to understand why their near-adult children were doing what they were doing, an LP record of sacred chants, a description of spiritual centers around the United States, and a bibliography of spiritual readings. Steve would design the package.

Ram Dass's tour financed itself, and those who attended were told that if they sent fifty cents to Lama Foundation, they would receive a package of teachings. Steve and about six others worked in the Lama library for months creating pages for the core book; the manual for parents became an autobiographical sketch of Ram Dass's transformation from a successful Harvard professor in psychology to a devotee of Guru Neem Karoli Baba; and Sarada and others recorded chants to be mastered onto an LP.

Steve worked out the logistics of print production in Albuquerque, including the challenge of using kraft paper in a newsprint press, which hadn't been done before, at least not in New Mexico. Signatures of the core book, titled *From Bindu to Ojas*, were tied together at Lama with brown string, and all the contents were loosely placed in a sized and printed cardboard box, secured with the same string. We mailed these out from San Cristobal, in a form no post office would accept today. In the meantime, we were receiving hundreds of checks for fifty cents and hundreds of envelopes with two quarters and a name and address.

As the boxes were being mailed out, Ram Dass and Steve conferred about Ram Dass's need for greater funding for his work of spreading the teachings he had received. This was when *Be Here Now* was conceived. The content would be the same. Steve designed the cover and the additional pages, and a distribution contract was arranged with Crown Publishers. The price of $3.33 was also Steve's idea. We thought hard about whether to print five or ten thousand copies and decided to take a chance and print ten thousand. The publication date was April 2, 1971. In September 1979 the book had its twenty-third printing, for a total of well over half a million copies. I have lost track since then.

I feel that any attempt to describe my experience and view of Lama Foundation in full would be like trying to describe a whole world. Structured as it was, most of those in other communes regarded it as a rather uptight place. It was implicit that the only real reason for being there was for awakening consciousness—in other words, for spiritual development. But in the process of living in community, a powerful teaching in itself, there were many inevitable struggles and heartbreaks. My marriage to Frances ended there, as did Steve's with Barbara, and between us there were seven children to care for. Many people came, thinking to escape—and carrying with them the baggage from which they were fleeing. There was and remains an ongoing tension between the needs of the community and the needs of the individual. Eileen and Peter Caddy, founders of Findhorn, stated while visiting Lama that living in community was a fine way to sand off the rough edges. In short, living at Lama was beautiful and terrible, inspiring and heartbreaking, and anything but "roses, roses." My heart was broken there many times, and yet I remain grateful.

One of Herman Rednick's sayings that I still take to heart is "The essence of spirituality is practicality at all levels." It felt to me that this was part of what we were trying to realize at Lama and why I wanted to be there, the face of heartbreak.

There's a lot yet unsaid: the many, many teachers of many traditions who came, who taught, and who honored the community with their teachings; Flag Mountain prayer flags, initiated by Steve and Barbara as Lama's first cottage industry; the publications of *The Bountiful Lord's Delivery Service*, led by Ahad Cobb; weddings and funerals; births and burials; the grave of Murshid Samuel Lewis, who once wrote that at Lama, "they practice, practice, practice what others preach, preach, preach"; the beginnings of the summer retreat program, suggested and facilitated by Steve, already then called Nooruddeen; a number of severe crises of personality, marriage, ideology, fire, and flood and the strength of the tradition of governance in the face of these crises; and the magic of community when it is really felt as such, a state of collective consciousness for which institutional structure affords only a prop and a possibility.

It is the realization of that collective consciousness toward which, I think, the counterculture aspired but which, I believe, requires work on oneself at the individual level. Lama Foundation helped me immensely in that direction. It changed my life.

Steve is now Nooruddeen, a Sufi sheikh devoted to the Shadhuliya order; Frances is now Noura Issa, Steve's wife; Barbara is now Asha Greer, an artist and part of the leadership circle of Murshid Sam's lineage, the Sufi Ruhaniat International; I am teaching as a semiretired faculty member of St. John's College and live with Sakina, my wife of thirty-nine years. We have moved on—but I still hope and pray that Lama Foundation will continue to awaken consciousness, to break and open hearts, and to help people become more fully human.

Double rainbow over Lama. Photo courtesy of Siddiq Hans von Briesen.

8

A New Buffalo Vision

ART KOPECKY

ONCE WHEN I WAS ABOUT TWENTY YEARS OLD, I was in midtown Manhattan about 5 p.m., surrounded by a gigantic flood of people as the office towers disgorged their occupants. "How precarious is our civilization, how precarious these people's lives," I thought. They get everything they need with money, and if that money stops flowing into their account, they are almost immediately desperate, truly desperate. Our society is almost hysterically, continually trying to grow when it is already too big, to keep the money flowing, finding something for all the people to do.

These thoughts, among other things, propelled me to step onto and into the near pristine, wide-open spaces of northern New Mexico. I had been in "Bezerkeley" for a while, then Bolinas on the California coast in a communal household where I paid the rent ($50 a month) and we housed many of these floating people, the Hippie People, as some called us. Then came travels, Ken Kesey–style, in a psychedelic Wonder Bread truck. We traveled north to several communities (communes), Rainbow Farm near Drain, Oregon, and the 365-acre Crow Farm near Eugene. Then we went east across Montana to another stay on a piece of land in Minnesota. From there we set our sights on the warmer Southwest. One day Pepe said, "Load the tipi," and our little troop, about ten people, headed south to find adventures in the Land of Enchantment.

Paula knew someone in Taos, so we went there, and before long we were directed to Black Rock Hot Springs on the edge of the rushing Rio Grande, deep in a gorge. And from there we were invited by a naked girl sitting in the warm water to partake of dinner at the New Buffalo commune. This was the hardscrabble farm nearest to where the Arroyo Hondo valley narrows and its little river cuts down into the gorge. I was soon running deer trails up and down the sides of the valley through piñon and juniper trees, through desert sage and chamisa, in a landscape that could have existed ten thousand years ago.

Over the previous five years, I had traveled from the canyons of New York City to the canyons of New Mexico, where nature reigns in all its beauty. For this I gave thanks.

We parked at New Buffalo and remained. Here was a very earthy outpost built in the old style of handmade adobe bricks and great round logs harvested from the

Top left: *Art Kopecky, 2016. Photo by Jack Loeffler. Bottom left: "Live the Dream, Live in Community," Art Kopecky near Sebastopol, California. Photo by Art Kopecky.* Right: *New Buffalo, 1970s. Photo courtesy of Seth Roffman.*

ponderosa pine forest. The central kiva was partly dug into the ground, providing the original communards the dirt with which to fashion thousands of thirty-pound adobe bricks. With a raised fire pit in the center and an earthen bench around the perimeter, this, the circle room, had a mystic aura, both ancient and futuristic. New Buffalo was serving one of its prime functions, as a refuge, and as a leading edge of an amorphous cultural revolution. So we had found what we were looking for without even knowing where it existed.

This remarkable dwelling had been built for "us." Oddly, all the original pioneers had left. They had been caught up in the "Summer of Love" Aquarian flash of higher consciousness that revealed itself to a sizable group of people. Then, living too primitively and unsure of how to proceed, the originals gradually began to depart from New Buffalo. It seemed appropriate that our little group should add our enthusiasm and wisdom to give this grand notion of sharing and living cooperatively a further evolution. Eventually many of the originals, like Max Finstein, Daddy Dave, and Larry McInteer, found their way back and continued to help further this experiment.

Erecting a tipi, New Buffalo, 1970s. Photo by Seth Roffman.

"Back to the land in cooperative culture" we now call it. And here it was happening, a very spontaneous gathering, and what could become of it was entirely up to us. This seemed magical, in a magical setting.

It was the fall of 1971 when Pepe and I, Carol with baby Kachina, Kiva, Suzie, Ray, Paula and son Sierra Nanda, and others adopted New Buffalo as our new home. The little pueblo had at least sixteen different bedrooms. Many were not occupied. Extending west from the central kiva were three rooms plus a round tower room with a second-story loft. Also to the west were most of the forty acres of fallow fields. To the east, three more rooms were attached. And the view from this side was the rugged Sangre de Cristo Mountains, reaching to above thirteen thousand feet. Here was the idyllic panorama of purple mountains' majesty. To the north were the communal kitchen and washroom and the pantries. To the south was a separate bedroom/workroom, on the same level as the circle floor (where I eventually settled). From the air the pueblo could be seen to generally replicate the Zia symbol, which originated in the Zia Pueblo in New Mexico, invoking the ancient wisdom and connections to this land that could still be easily perceived as God's land. That is not a thought that would occur to one standing in midtown Manhattan, where I had been just five years before.

Tuning in to what needed to be done at the commune, wanting to be busy, I started to do runs for firewood. We didn't usually have a chainsaw, so hearkening to an earlier mode, we used double-headed axes and handsaws, including an impressive

Top left: *Cook shack at New Buffalo, 1970s. Photo by Seth Roffman.* Top right: *Meal at New Buffalo, 1970s. Photo by Seth Roffman.* Bottom left: *Constructing at New Buffalo, 1970s. Photo by Seth Roffman.*

two-man saw. There were some areas of natural piñon and juniper woodland that (sadly) were being denuded to encourage the grasslands native to this semiarid environment. We were guided to these areas to scrounge the basic fuel for cooking and heating. There was propane for hot water in the kitchen and the washroom, but all the cooking and heating were done with wood, as had been the practice for countless generations.

And keeping warm is a serious matter at this 7,000-foot elevation. After a storm clears and the universe is revealed in its near-impossible complexity and thrilling clarity, the temperature can drop to -30 degrees F.

These wood runs were heavy work, but I did them joyously, believing I was part of a movement that made so many contributions to solving humankind's problems. If this lifestyle proved viable, then many farms, ranches, and estates could adopt a sharing culture, and the human race could stop destroying nature and stop adding to the cities, stop adding suburbs and shopping centers. It seemed to me a desperate need. And here an answer was happening, so spontaneously, a manifestation of a group effort directed by some need in the culture for more love, more thought, more respect.

Though originally from New York, I had a propensity for farming. My folks did spend summers in Connecticut on a chicken farm in the beautiful New England

Morning Star crew coming to visit New Buffalo, 1969. Photo courtesy of the Lisa Law Production Archives.

countryside, and I seem to have a recessive peasant gene. I soon took note of the local community irrigation ditch, the Acequia Llano del Madre, which ran for three miles, giving water to eighty homesteads on the south side of Arroyo Hondo. New Buffalo was the last property on the ditch and had four concrete and wooden take-offs, which fed the denuded fields of New Buffalo. Snowmelt from the high mountains fed this river system, which is tapped at least five times to feed over five thousand acres. Where the water is first divided, above Valdes, for the Desmontes system, a large ditch seems to climb the sparsely vegetated valley slope. Farther down the river, in thick woods, a dam of tree parts and rocks diverts water toward Arroyo Hondo. A concrete-and-wood fixture can control the flow. In the winter the ditches must be shut off because the water, freezing into dams, will destroy the built-up side of the ditch.

I sometimes wished that I were a great orator—that I could persuade people, move people. But I wasn't. My thoughts were too gentle, too complex, or something. The crowds crave anger and blame—not my message. So I made up for that by setting an example of hard work. I took the name Livingproof, AnSwei Livingproof. I saw the possibilities of a prosperous farm where a dozen prairie dog colonies dominated the abandoned fields. By spring I was repairing ditches and running the water into the prairie dog tunnels, from hole to hole. And we continued the New Buffalo custom of planting an acre or two of wheat. And I saw that all the ranchers and the Indians planted alfalfa, and I was determined to see these fields turn green and lush.

At the same time, I was meeting the extended family. A great advantage of a "welcoming community" is that the world comes to you. The Hog Farmers and friends from Long John's Valley and the Seven Room House knew they could sleep in the circle by the fire and could join the big dinner that occurred every evening. From the north came fellow communards from Ortiviz Ranch, Libre, and the Red Rockers. The mountain men in leather and worn clothes and the beautiful women in free-store fashions fascinated me. Pepe took on the spirit of welcoming and loving all these brothers and sisters. And from the Taos Pueblo came Little Joe Gomez, Tellus Good Morning, Joe Sandoval, and others to pray in peyote ceremonies, wherein some members of the commune became devoted followers. A big tipi that could seat sixty people was passed around. New Buffalo's twelve-foot flatbed was often used to transport the sturdy poles. At times, several bands would set up in the circle or in the courtyard. There was no admission; there was no charge at dinner. Nothing has ever sounded better than Joe Coda on the honky-tonk piano. This indeed was a revolutionary economy. Still we participated in the regular economy too, and sometimes those collecting for the beer runs would give me a cut, knowing I would buy seed and dairy cows and pay some bills.

For years I worked for no pay to make this extended family prosper and to establish a business: first, candles and then a cow dairy business, which fit the land so well. And many others also gave of their love and labor. At university I was a student of history, and in my raised platform bed I thought of men and boys who had fought in the American revolution or for the Union in the Civil War, or I thought of the soldiers of the Soviet Union or the US in World War II—those who were willing, who got up and made a difference. And I thought how lucky am I whose task is to work for peace, not to kill and risk being maimed. To work where there are women and prosperity, to help a race, the human race, whose consciousness is just awakening.

I did not invent the idea of the "dawn of the Aquarian Age," the concept of "higher consciousness," or the notion of "commune." But I was ready for it. This "enlightenment" touched me and I knew this was my path. With no one looking, I would place my palms together and be thankful, for my health, my conviction, my luck.

Some very good years followed. Dunyan came along with a flatbed truck and beehives. Kim and PeggySue sold garden produce and made huge salads for us. Kerim bought a horse-drawn mower. I bought an Allis-Chalmers tractor, and Jessie and I drove it home. Price was $250. I had to owe Epimenio León $50, but I paid up when I was able. With the tractor we pulled the mower and a two-bottom plow, and a dump rake for making windrows. We threw seed by hand, making for a festive occasion. The famous movie *Easy Rider* portrays New Buffalo, where Dennis Hopper was sometimes a guest. The scene of barefoot folk spreading seeds is very true to life. So is the portrayal of the pre-dinner circle, when we gathered, held hands, and someone would say words of thanks and we would look at each other with great affection.

The tractor pulled a harrow, a flat steel contraption with short teeth and a log dragged behind to help bury the seed. When judged ready, the alfalfa hay would be cut, turned, and then picked up by pitchforks, another festive occasion, when many could help. An experienced member would carefully stack the hay on the flatbed truck, keeping the alfalfa leaves intact. Then again, carefully, the hay would be off-loaded in a corral at the barn, made into a giant long bread-loaf sort of stack ten or twelve feet tall. Then a hay knife, a sort of sword with two handholds, would slice the compressed hay. If done right, the cows would get served a near perfectly preserved bunch of alfalfa plants, which is the basis of the dairy. That stack was our gold. When covered with a tarp and snow, this city boy who rode the subways would admire it more than all the towers of the New York skyline.

Some things we got very right. The New Buffalo Corporation owned the land. It was a gift, so there was no expensive mortgage to make us concentrate on paying the bank. The compassion and love were abundant. For years this was a telling example of non-greed. It was the opposite of the greed that keeps the wealthy from sharing and helping the people. Ours was not a soapbox lamenting the state of things, but a living enterprise to make things right through our work. Besides dairy, some took up the Southwest jewelry trade. The need to earn money and pay our way we also got right. And we were open, not shut off in some paranoid vision of the evil state, like the horrendous Jonestown. The FBI or sheriff we welcomed, wanting to not cause fear. I was mayordomo of our ditch, an accepted member of officialdom. What we didn't get right was the lack of a membership process. Pepe and Daddy Dave were angry with me for suggesting it. Thus, in 1979, Sandy and I with two kids were expelled by Joe and John, who saw an opportunity to waltz in with guns and knives and take over just as the commune was starting to become prosperous. Too many had left, not trusting their lives to this way. Very few shared my vision.

Today, membership and explicit governance are basic to the more mature, still growing, communities movement. We all must harbor some hope for the future. Many Republicans believe lower taxes will spur economic growth to solve all problems. Those of us who dread more destructive growth must believe in something else. But believing in the power of government to solve all problems neglects to see how overburdened with costs the governments already are. So progressive people need something else. The communities movement is a gift, carried on by a small cadre of people waiting for the consciousness to develop, to surge again, to grasp this common cause and make it a firm pillar of our society. My friends and I helped lay some of that foundation, right here in New Mexico.

Bill and Athena Steen's early days at Canelo. Photo courtesy of Bill and Athena Steen.

9

In Search of a Better Way of Building

BILL STEEN

THE YEAR WAS 1989, when the end of my first marriage required me to either sell the land where we now live or buy out my former wife. While not exactly penniless, I was in no position to come up with that kind of money. I felt very dejected because the property that I had found in the oak woodlands of southeastern Arizona I had envisioned as a place where I could fulfill a vision I held for the remainder of my life. Despite the strength of my convictions to remain, I realized that one's dreams and visions can have their fickle moments, and I was left wondering if I had been carried away by misguided illusions. It was not an easy time.

By then, my current wife and partner, Athena, had come into the picture; we had been together for not much more than a year. She helped provide the extra bit of determination and encouragement that was needed to forge on ahead. With no foreseeable options on the horizon, we came up with the most impractical plan ever: build something even though realtors were showing the property. We began construction on what is now our small straw-bale guesthouse.

Inviting friends to join us, we organized a workshop that to our knowledge was the first ever for straw bale building. That workshop was magical and memorable. Athena was seven months pregnant; her mother, Rina, was there in support, along with fellow straw bale pioneers David Bainbridge, Matts Myrhman, and others. Not having much of a clue as to what we were doing, we relied upon what we had learned from some of the historic Nebraska straw-bale buildings and a "make it up as you go" approach. When the roof was finally completed, the walls were out of plumb and the window openings skewed. However, we had survived a week of heavy monsoon rains and the bales remained dry. We overcame these minor defects, and twenty-five years later, it remains a wonderful space. With a little love and care, there is nothing to suggest that it won't last another hundred years.

Athena's straw-bale history began a few years earlier than mine. When her family needed a place to live during the northern New Mexico winter, her father, Ralph Swentzell, then a tutor (professor) at St. John's College in Santa Fe, suggested that

Bill and Athena Steen preparing straw bales, present day. Photo courtesy of Bill and Athena Steen.

building with straw bales in winter would be easier than adobe. The little cottage served her family well for five years. Athena thought she had invented something totally new, and it wasn't until a few years later when I went to photograph that little house that she learned that other bale buildings had preceded her.

What brought us together and led us to explore a different way of building is a bigger story. Our connection was strong on many levels and ultimately took the form of our nonprofit organization, the Canelo Project, a vehicle for "Connecting People, Culture and Nature." It was our vehicle to explore ways of living that did no harm to the natural world, that allowed different cultures to learn from one another and explore new ways of living, growing food, and creating sustainable habitat. The dream was lofty, but, hey, without dreams, little ever changes.

When it came to building, we were in many ways a continuation of those who explored various forms of alternative construction in the late 1960s and early '70s. Buckminster Fuller was preaching geodesic domes, the Southwest gave birth to the passive solar adobe movement, builders from northern California and the Pacific Northwest pushed the boundaries of wood construction, while Lloyd Kahn published his cult classic book *Shelter*, which inspired people all over the world to rethink how habitat is created.

These different building movements did not happen independently. They were part of the much bigger picture called the counterculture, interrelated elements that were permeating and transforming mainstream society. It was like a stream of consciousness comprising many threads of concern that permanently changed life on this planet: the *Whole Earth Catalog*, meditation, Zen, astrology, ecological awareness, organic gardening, self-sufficiency, Dylan, the Beatles, LSD, marijuana, Atlantis, and much, much more.

In concert with these influences of the 1960s, Athena and I were fortunate to inherit the rich traditions of cultural continuity present in the Southwest that were made possible by Native American cultures and proximity to Mexico. We shared a love for the unique landscape, the ethnicity of the food, and traditional buildings. Our parents were of mixed cultural backgrounds. Our fathers had come from east of the Mississippi, while our mothers embodied the Southwest. Athena's mother was Native American from Santa Clara Pueblo in New Mexico; my mother's family was from rural Sonora, Mexico. Their cultural differences divided them but also enriched them. Consequently, we assimilated not only their challenges but also the lessons they had learned. We both grew up in adobe homes; my parent's home was a classic old-style, northern New Mexico adobe, while Athena shared in the experience of building her family's passive solar adobe home.

As the 1960s were passing, it became clear to me that I needed to take the best of that era and put it all together in a different way of living. The promises of great wisdom and enlightenment being suggested by the practices of meditation, yoga, and such disciplines were irresistible. I began an earnest practice of Kundalini yoga and joined a group of friends in northern New Mexico who were practicing the same yoga, growing an organic garden, and building with adobe. I couldn't imagine needing anything more.

After a short while, our group split apart and we moved close to the town of Española. Unexpectedly I found myself in charge of a yoga ashram. The short story is that I laid the foundations for Yogi Bhajan's mini-Sikh empire. The years ahead were mixed, some beneficial but much leading me down a path that I had never wanted to travel.

Within a few years, the excitement and passion I had initially felt for my new lifestyle had disappeared. It had become obvious that I wasn't going to get enlightened anytime soon. I found myself consumed by the bureaucracy of running a large ashram, part of a religion I never wanted to join. Worst of all, I felt totally disconnected from the ground beneath my feet. One of the main reasons I had gone to New Mexico was to build with adobe, and twelve years later I had barely touched the earth.

It was vividly clear to me that a life dedicated to spiritual pursuits without an understanding of how to live sanely on this planet was nothing but empty. I left the ashram life and returned to my roots, Tucson.

Not long after relocating to Arizona, I moved to the tiny town of Canelo, Arizona. There I felt at home. It was the borderlands of Arizona and Mexico, close to the birthplace of my maternal grandmother in Sonora and a culture that had been a huge part of my early childhood years.

I loved the property, but there were several old houses for which I had no use. The cost of tearing them down was prohibitive, so I decided to do some basic remodeling and then later build the house of my dreams. Some dreams don't include the bigger picture. Thirty years later I am still living in those buildings, the remodeling isn't finished and probably never will be, and, quite truthfully, I have no regrets. They became the heart of the Canelo Project and allowed us to carry on many activities that would have been impossible without them. With all their imperfections I have grown to love them, and our life continues to revolve around them.

Those old houses were my entry into the world of building. They were true to the vernacular of the area, adobe walls with corrugated metal roofs built with standard lumber. We carried that style over to our straw bale buildings, with one fundamental change. We substituted straw bales, with their higher insulation value, for the adobe walls. With the one and a half to two inches of clay plaster we used to cover the straw bales, we essentially added a total of four inches of mini adobe walls. The approach made sense: the materials needed weren't costly and were within the reach of most people. Better yet, what we envisioned could be local and made of the dirt from the ground: clay floors, plasters, paints, sculptural forms, even furniture. We were in sync with one another, enchanted by the possibilities but with one minor obstacle: we really didn't know what we were doing. Back then the "how" of straw bale building was pretty much guesswork and could be reduced to those who advocated load bearing versus post and beam. It was all pretty simplistic. Back then it was easier. People had more time, the cost of living was less, building codes weren't as stringent. The world of building was not so driven by speed, efficiency, and manufactured materials as it is now.

We believed in what we were doing and forged ahead. I think part of what inspired us was that despite the knowledge being gained by the building industry, everything was becoming increasingly expensive, often unnecessarily complex, and on the whole, quite shoddy. America was becoming saturated with buildings, perfectly engineered on paper, that were unattractive and built from materials no better than those used on the cheapest houses. Their lifespan was at best questionable. The Third World was increasingly dominated by concrete. The modern building bore little resemblance to the well-made buildings of the past. It was also the McMansion era, when houses continued to grow unnecessarily large and were totally out of proportion to people's needs. The consequence was that it became almost impossible to build from local materials because of the time required and the cost of labor. Adobe, the most sensible material for the arid regions of the world, became expensive and impractical.

Our book *The Straw Bale House* was what we hoped would be a reasonable alternative to what we witnessed around us. It was both a survey of what other straw-bale builders had previously done and our personal agenda for what we wanted to pursue. The question of how to begin was quickly solved. In writing the book, we spent whatever money we had, using up all sources of available credit, and there was no promise of any kind of income in the near future. Any book royalties that might come our way were far off. The University of Arizona and the Farmer-to-Farmer program came to our rescue. They made us a proposal: travel expenses, meals, and lodging to work for the Save the Children Foundation in Ciudad Obregón, Sonora, Mexico, the great wheat belt of Mexico, where there was an abundance of straw and a need for alternatives that reduced the burning of surplus straw. With no other offers on the table, we accepted.

Normally, a chance to work in Mexico would have been ever so enticing; however, Ciudad Obregón was not exactly the Mexico where we hoped to spend time. Designed in New York, the city was part of a scheme to sell agricultural land to foreign investors for growing new hybrid wheat. It was the birthplace and headquarters for the Green Revolution. Little did we know it was actually perfect. There were no building codes, and an abundance of straw and clay soils and a talented labor force were at our disposal.

Our arrival coincided with a devaluation of the Mexican peso; consequently the cost of cement went through the roof. Most construction came to a halt. After looking at families living in shacks made of corrugated asphalt sheets, scraps of wood, and cardboard, it was obvious that we could do better. We scraped together materials, in a pinch got someone to bale Johnson grass, used pallets to make the roof rafters, filled sandbags with gravel for the foundation, made a structural corset of bamboo, and plastered with clay. The cost was $300 for a comfortable one-room hut. It was a big improvement, if far from perfect.

We did several more small projects like this one, and then the opportunity came to build an office building for Save the Children. We developed a deep friendship with our Mexican co-workers and their families. We couldn't have done it without them.

The office building laid the foundation for our future work. In the process of building the 5,000-square-foot office, we explored almost every local resource. We harvested clay for plasters and paints from the surrounding area, we used carrizo, a reed that resembles bamboo, in the walls, the straw bales were produced nearby, and we slaked lime from Alamos for plaster and tried every possible roof configuration we could think of in an area where wood was not an option. Some things proved valuable, others not so much, but in the end, it was nothing short of exquisite. It was a statement of collaborative creativity made possible by the friendships we had made, the cultural mix of working, eating, having fun together. The reliance on local materials kept environmental impact to a minimum.

Over the years, we continued our explorations into the world of straw bales and clay, but those early years in Ciudad Obregón remained our foundation. Since then we have refined our straw-bale building methods. We have been fortunate to work with some very skilled and sophisticated clay craftsmen from Japan and talented craftsmen from Europe, Australia, and elsewhere, but in many ways that time in Mexico remains the most memorable, probably because it was there that they found a way of making something beautiful and the skills required were such that all those who applied themselves could do it. It didn't require a lifetime of training.

Today we live in a world that is more connected than ever via the Internet. In the course of human history, we have moved through tribalism and the development of religions and nation states, and ultimately we are on our way to biosphere consciousness as one human race. Can we overtake the negative by-products, the entropy of the past that has brought us together? I'm an optimist: I think we can. In the process, building will continue to change, perhaps dramatically. Now 3-D printers are producing houses. I suspect 3-D printers will even build with clay and other natural fibers and in the process keep environmental impacts to a minimum. Whatever the case, there will always be a place for the human hand to bring creativity and beauty to buildings in a way no machine will ever do.

10

Countercultural Taos: A Memoir

SYLVIA RODRÍGUEZ

FOR THE FIRST THIRTEEN YEARS OF MY LIFE, Taos was a slow, unchanging adobe town with no sidewalks and one paved road. Many homes and even the convent school I attended had no indoor plumbing. Farmers still drove horse-drawn plows and wagons. The Taos Plaza stood half a block east of Our Lady of Guadalupe Church and roughly four blocks south of our house. It was the heart of commercial, political, and social activity, where all the action took place: where people went to shop, to trade, to socialize, for politics and gossip, the picture show, a cantina, to rendezvous, to watch tourists. The Indian taxi to Taos Pueblo was stationed on the east side of the Plaza. My father had a drugstore on the north side. His father, a professional gambler from Chihuahua who dealt monte in the back room of a hotel on the south side long before I was born, had once operated a *carnicería*, or meat store, on the west side. The Taos of my childhood was roughly 86 percent Hispanic, 7 percent "Anglo," and 7 percent Pueblo Indian.

Sylvia Rodríguez. Photo courtesy of Sylvia Rodríguez.

Things began to change around 1960, when I entered my teens. The day the church burned stands out as a portent of transformation. One morning, smoke rose high in the air as I walked down Placita Road toward the Plaza. I was stunned to see it came from the church. Volunteer firemen worked all day to quench the flames, but the roof kept smoldering. Finally, after hours of watching, I stood with Eulalia Emetaz under the portal of La Galería Escondida across from the church when the steeple crashed to the ground. It was the most exciting day of my life, but nothing compared to what would come. Eulalia cried when the steeple fell. She was a close friend of my parents, proprietor of the first (exclusively) modern art gallery in Taos, and a recent Catholic convert.

She was also the primary source of my early exposure to bohemia. Bohemian Taos is an important part of this story because in some sense it laid the groundwork for the emergence of hippie Taos a few years later.

My mother had come to Taos in the early 1930s to escape upper-middle-class Austin society and study art. She lived a carefree bohemian life for a couple of years, then one day happened to meet my father at a drugstore soda fountain on the Plaza. They soon fell in love and married, crossing class, ethnic, and religious lines in a match that scandalized my father's conservative Catholic Hispano-Mexicano maternal family. The Trujillos had been in Taos for roughly two hundred years and went, in the space of a single generation after American incorporation, from farming their land to working for wages. My parents, poor lambs, had no idea what they were getting into, but that is another story. I grew up in the bosom of my father's extended family, on the fault line between different and largely separate cultures, classes, religions, and social worlds. In order to receive his mother's blessing for their marriage, they promised to raise their children as Catholics. Loretto nuns taught me to read and write and of course to pray. But my mother, raised Episcopalian and turned agnostic, planted the subversive seeds of skepticism that slowly took root and spread like rhizomes in the garden of my mind. Both my parents, in their radically different ways, reached beyond their native orbits and got their fingers burned. They ended up alcoholics but managed to hold their tattered nest together until he died, producing two daughters who have lived, each in her own way, against the grain.

Eulalia's mix of edginess, wit, charm, and warmth won her a special place in my parents' home, and by the time I entered my teens, she spent most holidays with us. She recruited me to pour what she called her special Taos Lightning punch at her gallery openings. There I met and served liquor to all of Taos's art world, made up of the last of the art colonists, the early modernists, and plenty of weirdos, left-wingers, and queers, as my father saw them. Lois Rudnick's biography of the Mabel Dodge Luhan house identifies utopianism as the common ground between bohemian and hippie countercultures. Mabel brought bohemia to Taos, and when she began to fade, the Helene Wurlitzer Foundation, directed by Henry Sauerwein, kept the gateway open to hundreds of artists who over the decades passed through its doors for a brief cottage sojourn. Like Mabel's guests, Wurlitzer grantees often became seasonal or permanent residents. Late bohemia shaded into early hippiedom.

The difference between bohemia and hippiedom was partly generational but also a matter of cultural emphasis. Bohemia centered on art and was fueled mostly by alcohol. Hippiedom centered on lifestyle and was fueled by hallucinogenic drugs. Both bohemians and hippies were antimodern, antiestablishment romantics who opposed war and idealized and emulated Indians. Both generations were shaped by war, racial conflict, economic change, class mobility, and social upheaval. The hippie counterculture arose among boomers during the Vietnam War on the heels of the civil rights movement and concurrently with the Black Power, Chicano, and American Indian movements. Its early phase was untouched by feminism. Political assassinations punctuated the era. Young men were faced with the terror of either evading or yielding to a military draft that fed directly into an escalating war machine. The dividing line was largely but not exclusively a matter of class. The early hippies were communitarians. They were environmentalist, primitivist back-to-the-landers, drawn to mysticism, supernaturalism, and Oriental religions, longings all abundantly nourished by hallucinogenic or psychedelic drugs. The whole swirling phantasmagoria came with a rock 'n' roll/Ravi Shankar soundtrack.

The Great Taos Hippie Invasion started in the summer of 1967 and went on for about four years. 1967 was also the year Reies López Tijerina and the Alianza Federal de Mercedes, or land grant movement, staged their famous Tierra Amarilla courthouse raid. The following year, university campuses across the country would erupt in antiwar protests met with violent police reprisals. Thousands of mostly white, mostly middle-class, young people began to pour into northern New Mexico, fleeing the corruption of cities and suburbs in search of a pristine altiplano utopia replete with Indians, earthen architecture, and the promise of spiritual awakening. Taoseños reacted to the sudden influx more or less according to socioeconomic position and age. Hippie displays of excess, transgression, and abandon shocked and threatened businessmen like my father. They feared that the hippies would kill tourism, which eventually proved untrue because hippies themselves would become a tourist attraction. Proper middle-class Hispanos willing to tolerate a few beatniks were aghast at the spectacle of hippie dress, drug use, loose morals, poor hygiene, *sin verguenza* (shameless) violation of sexual norms, and flagrant use of food stamps and free clinics.

Local citizens feared their children would be corrupted, which of course happened in a flash as soon as local youth and newcomers partied together. Such settings could also give rise to antihippie violence in the form of beatings, gang rapes, and arson. Perhaps for the first time since the 1847 revolt, when Taoseños murdered the first American governor and other Americanos, (a small sector of) Anglos were suddenly vulnerable to both targeted and random acts of Chicano violence. Anthropologist Estelle Smith describes how some hippies, including Hollywood actor Dennis Hopper, who was by then living in the Mabel Dodge Luhan house, departed from their "flower child" ethos of peace and love to arm themselves against Chicano gang aggression. Local youths who "crossed over" into hippiedom were considered a disgrace to their families. Some left town for the freedom of anonymity in California. Those who stayed or returned home were forever marked by their deviation.

At the height of the hippie "infestation," outraged businessmen and civic leaders tried to cancel the town's summer fiesta due to the three Ds: drugs, dirt, and disease.

Still, some locals rented old houses to hippies and even cautiously befriended them. A potent bond grew between hippies and some of Taos Pueblo's elderly and middle-aged "peyote boys" (a term used by disapproving Taos Pueblo traditionalists), who found themselves revered as gurus with easy romantic access to a pool of willing "hippie girls" drifting through the region's many communes. Some hippies joined an inter-ethnic peyote church known as the American Church of God. For a while some even imitated Indian accents. A few settled down and became lifetime devotees of the church.

In the summer of 1967 I had just completed my sophomore year at college in New York City, a place that, once seen, had pulled me like a giant magnet. After two years of intense cultural and environmental shock, I was ready to come home for the summer. I signed up for a University of New Mexico summer archaeological field school on a ranch north of Taos. My interest had also been piqued by a *New York Times* article about a spiritual commune planned for New Mexico ("to build a focal point of spiritual energy on the North American continent") by the same artists who had created a spec-tacular psychedelic art installation I saw at the Riverside Museum. So when the field school ended, I went looking, and it didn't take long to find them. The field school was housed at the D. H. Lawrence Ranch near San Cristobal, and it so happened that the small group who would found the Lama Foundation were renting a couple of cabins at a nearby ranch. They had purchased roughly one hundred acres of land a few miles to the northeast on the side of Lama Mountain, where some were living in a bus and several tipis. They were all in their late twenties and had taken a lot of LSD and other psyche-delics. As soon as I met them, I wanted to join their project.

Why? Because by the time I graduated from high school, I had read Aldous Huxley's *The Doors of Perception* and other writings about psychedelics and was eager to try some myself. The summer before college I sought out a couple of Taos's proto-hippies to ask their help in obtaining peyote. I brought home a little bag of dried buttons, ground them into powder that I packed into large gelatin capsules obtained from my pharmacist father (who knows what he thought?), and washed them down one morning with orange juice. The result was violent nausea, a hot flood of unbelievably awful tasting vomit, and a profound transcendental experience that forever changed how I saw and felt about the world. Like so many of my generation who had similar experiences, I became consumed with the desire to achieve that state permanently and to assimilate its ineffable noetic content into a way of life. And like others, I foolishly believed a permanent state of transcendental consciousness could be attained by taking more psychedelics. This fanciful notion led some individuals into serious trouble. I might have been one of them but for Lama.

Unlike all the other communes cropping up around Taos, the Lama Foundation had a No Drugs rule. This enabled my nevertheless very reluctant and conservative

Artisans at the Mabel Dodge Lujan house, Taos, 1970s. Photo by Seth Roffman.

father to give me permission to spend the rest of the summer there. Two other rules that roped Lama off from the hippie bacchanalia surrounding it were no visitors except Sunday and a two-week residential trial period. I happily performed strenuous physical labor outdoors all day long, slept on the ground in a tipi, and communed and chanted and bonded with the small group of Lama founders. A steady trickle of psychedelic illuminati and other New Age wanderers passed through Lama the two summers I ended up spending there. In retrospect it seems that only the utopian idealism of privileged middle-class youth could have buoyed me through those euphoric summers when I came to realize that psychedelic drugs were not the remedy for ordinary everyday unenlightened consciousness.

The principal founders of Lama were a charismatic young couple whose experience-based authority on the promise and limits of psychedelics was the only kind I was willing to hear. They and most of the other founding figures eventually converted to Buddhist, Sufi, or Hindu sects, followed gurus within those traditions, and devoted the rest of their lives to the spiritual quest. Lama itself underwent many internal conflicts, upheavals, and transformations over the ensuing decades, but it is one of the only hippie communes that still survive today. That, too, is another story, not mine to tell. My involvement with Lama lasted for three years. At the end of each drug-free hippie-lifestyle summer, I would button up and go back to school. I was a seasonal and somewhat closeted hippie. It took me perhaps a decade to work through and assimilate the psychological and intellectual implications of my early psychedelic experiences. During my twenties I believed I was passing through the university on my way to the revolution, but ultimately it turned out to be the other way around.

Many hippies eventually gave up trying to live off the land and left. Some were able to sell at a profit properties cheaply purchased from locals, who then watched the prices escalate exponentially with every subsequent turnover. Some went into business and reverted to a middle-class lifestyle mildly inflected with New Age values. Ultimately bohemia was absorbed into hippiedom, which, like every other sector, is discernibly stratified by class. Even today hippies remain a prominent part of Taos's social landscape. Taos gradually gentrified and attracted new waves of postmodern hippies, affluent amenity migrants, and retirees.

By 1980, most of the communes were gone and the Plaza was a theme mall for tourists. Its old social, commercial, and political functions were now scattered in new constructions along the highway south of town. Real estate prices for old adobes on land with irrigation rights skyrocketed. For every native who emigrated for work or school, two more affluent and educated newcomers arrived. The Hispanic demographic proportion slipped to 67 percent. Resentment simmered. In another decade marijuana was still popular but driven increasingly underground. Hallucinogens became hard to find and were slowly replaced by cocaine, heroin, crack, methamphetamine, and prescription drugs. Alcohol consumption remained ever popular, constrained only by an open-container rule on the Plaza. Grassroots mobilizations against developments that threatened traditional water supplies (rivers, acequias, springs) began to emerge through uneasy alliances between post-hippie environmentalists and local farmer-ranchers. By 2014, according to the US census, the Hispanic proportion had dropped another 10 percent, while American Indians held steady at about 7 percent and Anglos ("white alone") were at 36. The middle class had expanded across all ethnic groups, and Taos's social fabric had grown increasingly complex.

It is easy for aging boomers to wax nostalgic about those days. But one must also look back with irony and a touch of skepticism because, contrary to their (our) youthful sensation of accelerating through some kind of Aquarian evolutionary process toward an egalitarian, spiritually enlightened, peaceful, and ecologically balanced society, the country soon veered sharply to the right in an overall trajectory that hasn't stopped yet. Hippie and other dissident boomers of many stripes were—if not the first—perhaps the last American generation to believe the world was on the verge of a marvelous transformation into something better. Ha. Alas.

11

"Locura, lo Cura"—Hispano Perspectives of Counterculture New Mexico: An Autoethnography

ENRIQUE R. LAMADRID

LIFE IS THE PSYCHOLOGICAL BALANCE between spin and counterspin, a gyroscope on a string, not flying, not falling, steady as it hums in space, creating its own gravity. In the park by the zoo, I watch my three-year-old son Carlos playing "round and round" until he can no longer stand. He falls down on the grass laughing, watching the world continue to turn. In control, out of control. The natural mind flexes its limits, explores its boundaries, say doctor Weil and grandfather Lao Tsu. "*Locura lo cura*," says *hermano vato loco* Levi, for those curative altered states set us back on course and remedy madness. Culture likewise reproduces and corrects itself with its own countercurrents. Deep thinking and contrary actions are the province of youth, deeply entwined with human development. The emerging self explores and bonds on environment and culture. The young ask and expect more of what is and commit to what might be: their future selves, individual and collective, between cultures, languages, ecosystems.

At fifteen in 1964, I left New Mexico with family for high school and the ocean in California. Went with friends to a music/light show gathering of the Merry Pranksters in a rented theater in downtown Los Angeles, crazy kaleidoscope bus parked out front. "Can you pass the Acid Test?" read the sign with Uncle Sam pointing at me. Declined the LSD at the door: "What's that?" Fortunate to save myself years later for Hermit Rapids in the bottom of the Grand Canyon, the best place of all to watch history melt into geology! Returned to Albuquerque with tales of the fabled Pacific and newfound celebrity to establish the Río Grande Surfing and Yacht Club. Two generations later there are still members with rafts at the ready! Then on to UNM, English major in Ecuador, professors Walt Whitman and Gary Snyder, Pablo Neruda, and Ernesto Cardenal. In my senior year, I won the draft lottery (#10 of 365) and a one-way ticket to Vietnam. No way, *cabrones*.

In the grip of the madness, on a beautiful August afternoon in 1969, I imagined I could disappear, drop out and away from my troubles. Hitched a ride north of Taos to the profound Arroyo Hondo valley. I had heard rumors of New Buffalo but was totally unprepared for the scene that unfolded as I walked down the dirt road above

Enrique Lamadrid at his home in Albuquerque. Photo by Jack Loeffler.

the commune. In a field of ripe wheat below, a regiment of neatly tied sheaves stood ready for the march to the threshing floor and the granary. With sickles at rest, a group of reapers relaxed on the ground, passing around jugs of water. It was a scene straight out of paintings by Bruegel and Van Gogh. I was ready to volunteer, but the day's work was already done. The reapers invited me to a meal of garbanzos, summer squash, tomatoes, and bread from their own wheat and flour! I uncorked and passed around a bottle of wine. The night sky was spectacular. They lent me a blanket and pointed out an empty tipi on a ridge nearby. No time for talk and not much sleep, for a woman was in labor that night and everyone was ready to help out. With the dawn, more bread and a hike to the Río Grande gorge, down to the hot springs. Back in the tipi, a small group sat and listened to a reading from the Psychedelic Verses, a free translation by Timothy Leary himself of the *Tao te Ching*, the book of the way, of wisdom in action.

> All things pass
> A sunrise does not last all morning
> All things pass
> A cloudburst does not last all day
> All things pass
> Nor a sunset all night

But Earth . . . sky . . . thunder . . .
wind . . . fire . . . lake . . .
mountain . . . water . . .
These always change
And if these do not last
Do man's visions last?
Do man's illusions?
Take things as they come
All things pass

An early afternoon rain squall blew down from Taos Mountain and made a perfect double rainbow to go with the poem. I said almost nothing, nor was told anything. With a nod of appreciation, I made an Irish exit and ambled back to the highway. Like a waking dream. There was something deeply authentic, profoundly hip about the communards—as if they had taken vows of poverty or self-sufficiency and commitment to the land. They had left their door open to newcomers. It was accessible, but just beyond my grasp. They were self-chosen children of the earth, but everyone was from somewhere else. *Extranjeros todos*. My amazement was tinged by misgiving. How could *la gente*, local *nativos*, fit into this vision? As smoothly as Jerry García?

Back in Burque, in spite of itself, the counterculture was being swallowed by the familiar American devotion to celebrity and consumerism. If there were messages in the music, which albums were most strategic for a low budget? Who were the coolest bards and music masters, Brubeck, Dylan, the Beatles or the Stones? Richard Fariña and Mimi Baez seemed most transformational, but what about all the rest? Nonconventionalism became a shopping list of music, clothes, attitudes, even food. Never tasted granola until 1969, hmm, pretty good. Then came *Whole Earth Catalog!* And finally our own transcontinental saga, the movie *Easy Rider*.

Up in Taos, bohemianism was burgeoning, since forever, just as with Mabel and D. H. in the 1930s. But who were the bohemians? Not the poor painters, struggling writers, maverick directors, or wannabe mountain men looking for the lowest rents with the best views. Turns out the bohemians were not even from Bohemia. The cheapest rents in nineteenth-century Paris were on the right bank near Montmartre in the Romani neighborhoods, as in Puccini's *La Bohème*, which inspired the rock musical *Rent* on Broadway in the 1990s. In Paris, everybody thought the gypsies were from Bohemia. Probably never bothered to ask. The picturesque locals were decoration, an exotic part of the backdrop, on the sidelines. Just as in New Mexico. Meanwhile the rents started going up and never did level off. After Dennis Hopper's *Last Movie*, in Taos things began to get edgy. He started packing a *pistola*, just as in the movies, right? *¡Cuidado!*

After Wavy Gravy and the Hog Farm fed the hungry and ran their Bad Trip Clinic at Woodstock, a multitude of seekers and beat campers showed up in Peñasco looking for the parties in Llano and Ojo Sarco to see what was going on. Some just passed through; others got on food stamps to spend the winter. At least the legendary annual baseball game between Picurís Pueblo and the Hippies broke the tension. But what about local Chicanos, or "Orcs," as some of them called us? We called them "Cool Arrows" in return, because they were so crazy about the indios. Many hippies fell in love with northern New Mexico, but the perils were many. For several summers running, people died from chewing water hemlock root. The deadly plant grows along high mountain streams right next to sacred *oshá*, the powerful mountain celery. The white composite flowers look identical. Only local knowledge, local culture, can save your life in the Sangre de Cristos.

In 1968, the year after the famous Tierra Amarilla courthouse raid, land grant guru Reies López Tijerina went to Mabel's old mud palace to meet with Hopper. Perhaps art should be an experience rather than an object? Tijerina decided to visit the communes and engage the hippies. To bridge cultural gaps was a strategy to mobilize potential allies for his campaign for New Mexico governor. In #11 of his twelve-point platform, he promises "to recognize and protect the rights of hippies and all of those who want to maintain their own personal lifestyle." Wow . . . ¡ay, ay, ay!

In Española, the courageous journalists of the bilingual newspaper *El Grito del Norte* reported on the national movement against the Vietnam War and the regional struggle for the land grants and published corridos, traditional protest ballads. Editorials encouraged peace with the hippies. But they insisted the "return to the land" could be problematic in the context of the struggle of Hispanos and Natives for the millions of acres of land lost in the biggest broken treaty of all: Guadalupe Hidalgo, 1848.

Utopian enthusiasm, political activism, and cultural revolution were a heady mix. But more than the shadow of the Vietnam War and social unrest complicated the counterculture in New Mexico. The people of our twice-conquered land live out a double colonial legacy. As a colonial enterprise, New Mexico began as a celebrated missionary province, achieved independence as a remote and impoverished Mexican state, and is now a prosperous military colony of the United States, with a sizable underclass to support its wealth. In 1848, the border of Mexico moved more than five hundred miles south, from the Arkansas River in southern Colorado, to the Río Grande at El Paso. In this broad Border Zone, language and identity are negotiated in every social encounter. How to communicate if your language has been subordinated? Cultural resistance becomes a survival strategy. We live between languages and cultures in asymmetrical relations of wealth and power.

Massive language loss occurred in New Mexico after World War II. If they were lucky, Indo-Hispano New Mexicans became English-dominant bilinguals. Native languages and Spanish had no more place in public discourse. They were considered simply impolite. Thanks to the renewal of counterculture in the 1960s and '70s, multiculturalism emerged, turned the tables, and romanticizes rather than denigrates cultural others. Now we celebrate our bilingualism. As the love song asks, "Hey baby, *¿qué pasó?*" Cultural hybridity is the norm. But the theme and traditional norm of the New Mexico History Museum continues to be "Culture in Place," a static view of history in which the twenty-first-century status quo is viewed as natural order. In an arid bioregion, rights to place are highly contested. People valiantly struggle to define and keep their places.

The cultural complexities of New Mexico are dynamic and fascinating. Mary Louise Pratt lists the literate arts of the Border Zone: "autoethnography, transculturation, critique, collaboration, bilingualism, meditation, parody, denunciation, imaginary dialogue, vernacular expression." The counterculture has validated and elevated all of these genres. They are best taught by "exercises in storytelling; identifying with the ideas, interests, histories, attitudes of others; experiments in transculturation and collaborative work and in the arts of critique, parody, and comparison . . . the redemption of the oral; ways for people to engage with suppressed aspects of history . . . ways to move into and out of rhetorics of authenticity; ground rules for communication across lines of difference and hierarchy that go beyond politeness but maintain mutual respect; a systematic approach to the all-important concept of cultural mediation." The road to knowledge and practice of the future was not straight or narrow. It was full of potholes, and every step was a calculated risk. Perils awaited at every turn.

For me, in June of 1970 things got worse as they got better. When my draft notice arrived a week after I graduated, I had to get out of town. I hitched north with just a light jacket, matches, fishing gear. A pickup stopped. I got in with a lively wavy-haired guy with owlish glasses who immediately started talking to me in Spanish. Tomás Atencio on his way to Embudo. A total stranger figured me out in no time. "Your daddy, Enrique Lamadrid, was my

Enirique Lamadrid at Ramah, 1971. Photo courtesy of Enrique Lamadrid.

favorite junior high teacher in Santa Fe. I met you when you were two!" He invited me to his *ranchito* in El Dique (Dixon) to help plaster his torreón and share conversation, beer, and posole. The torreón is a defensive tower, the New Mexico equivalent of the Spanish castle tower. "Our culture, our water, our land is under siege, so I thought I'd better build one," he winked.

We talked into the night and most of the next day, while we worked. Neighbors and friends dropped by to lend a hand. A guitar surfaced for lunch with a corrido or two. Counterculture, Nuevomexicano style, swirled all around us. There was idealistic talk about the new community-based think tank, La Academia de la Nueva Raza, and the oral history projects it was conducting. The *nueva raza* was the "new humanity" that Che wrote about so eloquently, the piquant mix of activism and culture that was emerging across the Americas. The foundation was the lively Socratic dialogue Atencio called *resolana*, named for the sun-drenched place, usually near the plaza, where people gathered to reflect and converse. This public space where critical community dialogue is cultivated is a direct descendant of the agora of ancient Greece. Never knew we were such *clásicos*.

The challenge was that most New Mexico plazas were gentrifying into tourist hot spots and the locals had to find other gathering places. Hermano David García has found them. Not yet so in Dixon, as I found out a few years later, when I stopped by for a visit on what happened to be a November election day. Since bars were closed and liquor sales were prohibited, I stumbled across a full-blown resolana on the *placita*, exactly 200 feet away from the polling place, as prescribed by law so as not to harass or influence voters. Wall-to-wall political jokes and discussions of candidates and issues were animated by several jugs making the rounds of the best bubbling apple cider I have ever tasted. ¡*Suave*!

In those days, my *camarada* Estevan Arellano was busy editing and distilling the Academia's oral histories, which inspired his own writing on picaros, those contrary countercultural trickster types whose ambition was not to work. They lived by their wits on the edges of society, and their penchant for satire and social critique kept them in perpetual trouble. The picaresque was one of my passions. Navajo friends had told me about the adventures of Coyote (in winter of course). I had read the *Satyricon*, the misadventures of two young friends who roamed the Roman empire during its most decadent times. I knew about the starving boy hero of *Lazarillo de Tormes* and its scathing critique of Golden Age Spain, with beggars on the streets despite all the gold of México and Perú in the king's treasury. I was so hard core, I even read the *Periquillo sarniento*, nicknamed for its own "itchy parrot" hero, whose hilarious exploits exposed the decadence of New Spain in the years prior to the wars of independence. In my studies, I mistakenly assumed that the picaros were literary and belonged to the past. Estevan showed me otherwise and introduced me to a few.

The most famous of them all, *"el Gonito,"* joined us the next spring for an expedition to the hills to find suitable cedar stumps and branches for Estevan's remarkable wood carvings. We headed out up the canyons in an ancient pickup with a saw and a couple of *seises* (six-packs). I was treated to the most amazing display of verbal virtuosity I had ever heard in Spanish, *el español nuevomexicano*. Our regional language has as much seventeenth-century archaic vocabulary as it does neologisms, recently coined from English. Code-switching between the two languages with Gonito was an art form. Estevan expertly captured these dialogues in his novel *Inocencio: Ni siembra, ni escarda, pero siempre come el mejor elote* (Innocence: He neither sows, nor hoes, but always eats the best ears of corn), which won important literary prizes in Mexico but is virtually unknown here. It is New Mexico's own authentic contribution to the millennial tradition of Ibero-American picaresque. I never knew Gonito's real name—Feligonio Sánchez—until after his passing in fall 2015. He was a beloved figure up north.

Millennial knowledge is imbedded in language, and the religious, historic, and satirical verses collected by the Academia were overflowing with it. One alabado hymn from the Penitente brotherhood praises the cycles of life and the earth:

De la tierra fui formado	From earth I was created,
la tierra me da de comer,	the earth gives me what I eat,
la tierra me ha sostenido	the earth has sustained me
y al fin yo tierra he de ser.	and in the end I will be earth.

The *hermanos* are the only Christian faithful I have ever seen who totally prostrate themselves (as deeply as Muslims) to venerate Holy Mother Earth, Santa Madre Tierra.

The lovely songs and impassioned speeches of *Los Pastores*, the traditional Christmas plays, are full of cultural contestation. At the urging of angels, the shepherds take the devil-infested road to Bethlehem to become the first conversos, the first Jews to convert to Christianity. A whole week before the Three Kings, the pastores show up on Christmas Eve and stage the epiphany of common people. Recited to dissuade the shepherds, the speeches of Lucifer, fallen angel of light, come straight down from the classic Spanish baroque poetry of Luis de Góngora:

Aprended, flores, de mí,	Learn, flowers, from me,
lo que va de ayer a hoy,	what passes from yesterday to today,
que ayer maravilla fui	yesterday I was a marvel and
y hoy sombra de mi no soy.	today I'm not even a shadow of myself.
Mando el sol, mando la luna,	I command the sun and moon,
mando ese cielo estrellado.	I command that starry sky.

El sol se verá eclipsado	The sun will be eclipsed
tan solo que yo le mande.	upon my command.

Even though he has the power to move mountains, stir the wind, and cause eclipses, Lucifer bemoans his defeat and yields to San Miguel, the archangel.

Among the "treasures" collected by Alejandro López and other Academia associates, one of the most amazing is an old Nuevomexicano *trovo*, or satirical contest poem. Disruptive political and economic forces are personified into comic characters. In *El Trovo del Atole y el Café*, the distinguished international figure of "lord Coffee" squares off with virtuous and nutritious "sister Atole," the humble blue corn gruel, who heals the sick and springs from the earth through honest labor rather than money:

Atole:	Corn Gruel:
Yo también soy el Atole	I am also Corn Gruel
y aquí te hago la guerra.	and here I do you battle.
¡Qué bien mantengo a mi gente	How well I maintain my people
con sólo labrar la tierra!	for only working the land!
Y tú, Café orgulloso,	And you, proud Coffee,
que sepa el mundo entero,	may the whole world know,
sacrificas a mi gente	you make my people sacrifice
de comprarte con dinero.	to buy you with money.

The virtuous Atole defeats the elitist Coffee and wins the battle of words, restoring honor and virtue to local culture over international commerce. The colorful counterculture of the twenty-first century and the Occupy (and De-Occupy) mobilizations against globalized economies share the same values.

In conclusion, my search for the most authentic self, the deepest culture, the most humane politics, leads full circle back to *querencia*, to homeland, both father and mother land, Nuevo México. As I began my professional work to link traditional culture to bioregion, the natural environment in which it takes root, I realized that counterculturism is a transnational legacy and an intangible legacy of all humanity. It is not a consumer fad, but the way that human beings, through their youth, open new roads to the future.

My professional travels, research, and teaching led to Mexico, which of course has its own bohemian traditions. I had already stumbled across pachucos early on in Albuquerque, those beat zoot-suiters and their new way of talking, *simón*. A few friends and I folded up our collars and walked the Cantinflas walk with taps on our shoes, down the junior-high hallway, until we got busted. Then there were those *bohemios* who hung out in cantinas, drank Bohemia beer, and listened to mariachis. In the 1980s, I was not really surprised to run across Mexicano hipsters, members of La Onda, the Mexican "new wave," spawned at its own foundational bilingual rock concert in 1971. With a mass ritual gathering, half a million strong at a farm in Avándaro, Mexico, experienced their own Woodstock, and the *roqueros* began singing in Spanish.

The country was in shock from its own guerrilla wars and the student massacre at Tlatelolco, during the 1968 Olympic Games. It was the year that united the youth movements of the world. Along with the desperate politics came the uplift of expanding consciousness. Thousands made the obligatory pilgrimage to Huautla, the mountain town in Oaxaca where the celebrated and unassuming magic mushroom lady, María Sabina, opened eyes and changed many lives. Hermano Mike rode up a forty-mile, twelve-hour road to find her. She looked deep into his eyes to see what kind of healing he required, and she pulled three "*derrumbes* (landslides)" and four "*santo niño* (holy child)" mushrooms from her basket. All night long, he listened to her gentle laughter as she sang to the saints, mocked her celebrity visitors, and prayed to the spirit of Benito Juárez.

As in New Mexico, Mexican bohemianism thrived in the 1930s before the conflagration of World War II. In 1938, French surrealist André Breton joined the salon scene of Diego Rivera and Frida Kahlo. Leon Trotsky was part of it after he was granted political asylum for his stance against the institutionalization of the Russian Revolution. His belief in the Revolution within the Revolution extended to art. With Breton and Rivera, he collaborated in a key manifesto, *Pour un art révolutionnaire indépendent*, an artistic Declaration of Independence for art, which also needs to keep evolving to maintain its revolutionary impact. Artists can contribute to the revolution, not through political conformity but through creative individuality. A quarter-century later, Che echoed these positions to protect artistic expression in Cuba.

To complete their work, Diego, André, and Leon sought solace in the tiny town of Erongarícuaro, on the shores of Lake Pátzcuaro. In the lake and mountain villages of Michoacán, the same devils, angels, and shepherds of New Mexico's Pastores plays wear fanciful carved-wood masks. Mexican folk culture is one of the reasons Breton declared Mexico "a surrealist country by nature." If he had made it to

Enirque Lamadrid, Mexico City, 1970s. Photo courtesy of Enrique Lamadrid.

Taos, he would have encountered the same "convulsive beauty." We like to think that he would have included New Mexico in the same vanguard cultural geography.

One of the key and most surreal moments in my own cultural pilgrimage was sitting in the congenial company of students and colleagues from New Mexico on the little dock in front of the very house in Erongarícuaro where Breton made his famous declaration. Our feet dangling in the water, we watched a faint Halley's Comet rise in the dark sky over Lake Pátzcuaro. Both Lucifer and Archangel San Miguel were hovering close by.

Sources

Arellano, Estevan. *Inocencio: Ni siembra, ni escarda, pero siempre come el mejor elote.* México: Grijalbo, 1992.

Atencio, Tomás. *Entre verde y seco.* Embudo, NM: Academia de la Nueva Raza, 1972.

Atencio, Tomás, E. A. Mares, and Miguel Montiel. *Resolana: Emerging Chicano Dialogues on Community and Globalization.* Tucson: University of Arizona Press, 2009.

García, David F. *La Resolana: Tracing the Communicative Cartographies of Gathering Spaces in North Central New Mexico.* PhD dissertation. Austin: University of Texas, 2015.

Lao Tzu. *Tao te ching.*

Leary, Timothy. *Psychedelic Prayers after the Tao Te Ching.* New Hyde Park, NY: University Books, 1966.

Pratt, Mary Louise. "Arts of the Contact Zone." *Profession 91*: 33–40. New York: MLA, 1991.

Romero, Levi. *In the Gathering of Silence.* Albuquerque, NM: West End Press, 1996.

Thomas, Michael A. *Headlight.* Novel, unpublished.

Weil, Andrew. *The Natural Mind: A Revolutionary Approach to the Drug Problem.* Boston: Houghton Mifflin, 2004.

Acknowledgments

Gracias, como siempre, a David García, los Migueles (Thomas y Gandert), Levi Romero, y Jack Loeffler.

12

Lowcura: An Introspective *Virtual Cruise* through an American Subcultural Tradition

LEVI ROMERO

. . . nostalgia gleams with the dull brilliance
of a chrome airplane on the rusted hood
of a '56 Chevy
. . . daydreams of walking bare foot
on the soft grass
down by the river
where dragonflies buzzed all day
have now decayed like the fallen cottonwoods
along the gnarled paths
of the Rio Embudo
where free form poetry
mixed with cheap beer
on warm nights by the riverbanks
and stories of lowered '49 Fleetlines
with flamejobs and spinners
were cast into the dark wind . . .

Hearts and Arrows

Years later, I would hear stories

I remember it this way, Magdalena. As a small child I would accompany my grandmother on her walks to and from my mother's house, which was about a mile and a half away. We would follow a walking path along the Río Embudo, a small stream weaving along the northern edge of the village where I grew up. There was a certain place along this walk that we always looked forward to. It was there, just off the sand and gravel trail under the shade of the towering cottonwoods and heavy scent of river willow and summer heat, where we would stop for a short respite. It was at this section along the river where some of the villager's discarded automobiles sat in abandonment, a sort of village car cemetery. One car in particular attracted our attention,

Levi Romero at his home in Dixon, 2016. Photo by Meredith Davidson.

a faded pink 1949 Chevrolet Fleetline flipped over on its back and succumbing to the rust and ruin of cars that meet such a fate. Grandma would walk over to it, and we would stand there momentarily, our hands caressing the fat-fendered Chevy. *"Este era el carro del Levi"* she would say, pointing to her grandson's car. We would silently pay our respects and move on. Years later, I would hear stories about my cousin Levi and his lowered Fleetline and learn that he had been one of the first Lowriders in northern New Mexico, the region around Española that in time became regarded affectionately as the "Lowrider Capitol of the World."

Resuello y Alma

I began cruising when I was about twelve years old with some older cousins who would take me along on their nightly cruises into town. It was in the early 1970s and the beginning stages of lowriding in Española. The factions between the Hotrodders and the Lowriders were visibly displayed under the streetlight's glow of shopping-center parking lots and along Main Street. My cousin li'l Joe recently moved back from California, had brought his passion for lowriding with him and transplanted it into the quickly forming, popular pastime. Li'l Joe would pass on down to me my first Lowrider, a copper brown 1959 Chevrolet station wagon with velvet curtains, shag carpeting, and a donut steering wheel. Truthfully, I never replaced the dead battery in the car and was never able to take it out on the cruise. Nonetheless, I'd accompany my cousins into Espa', usually cruising with my cousin Raymond in his dropped 1955 Chevy pickup truck. It was a beautiful piece of nostalgia painted a Diamond Black, rolling on baby-moon chromed rims on gangster-wide whitewall tires, with hood-mounted dummy spotlights and Bob Dylan on his stereo. And so, Magdalena, there begins my story—my earliest recollections of Lowriders and some of my first experiences and observations from within the breath and soul, *resuello y alma*, of a distinct American subcultural tradition, Lowriding.

Eran en los dias de Los Heroes

The Lowrider has always been a representation of individual expression and identity, with connotations of a rebellious and nonconforming nature. The vato loco archetype became the model for the Lowrider, and it was that paragon of social deviance that formed the alluring quality that sometimes attracted a young Chicano feeling the need to affirm his individuality and social status. In my contemplations regarding the Lowrider lifestyle, as I have witnessed it and lived it, as I have loved it and have attempted to outgrow my attraction to it, with no success, I have come to recognize that the Lowrider not only bore the burden of his own individual identification but also sustained the cultural traditions of language, religion, spirituality, allegiance to community, proclaiming proudly, even arrogantly, his existence in the reality of a social status smirked at by the status quo. I can recall as a young boy seeing these individuals parked in their lowered rides under the shade down by the river or along roadside turnarounds or cruising slowly through some dirt road weaving through the village, their slow rides bouncing rhythmically to the grooves spilling out from their car radios.

Los Heroes
los watchávamos
cuando pasaban
echando jumito azul
en sus ranflas aplanadas
como ranas de ojelata

eran en los días
de los heroes
cuando había heroes
turriqueando en
lengua mocha
y riza torcida

Q-volé

ahora nomás pasan
los recuerdos
uno tras del otro
y mi corazón
baila

bendición

bendición es
estar contento

Señor, gracias por . . .

gracias por todo

Por Vida

"always on the outside of whatever side there was when they asked him why it had to be that way well, he answered, just because"—"Joey," Bob Dylan

For any Lowrider, his car may be the ultimate form of expression and representation of how he views himself and wants to be seen, but the story would be incomplete if one were to showcase the Lowrider only through the marvelous and beautiful creation of the customized car. I believe, Magdalena, that the last thing in poetry is the poem, as I also believe that the last thing in lowriding is a lowered ride. The defining essence of what makes someone a Lowrider is something that cannot be relegated down to a material possession. In many instances, individuals who did not own a car or have a driver's license or the means to earn the wages that enabled them to possess and maintain a cool ride were those who best upheld the ideal image of what it was to be a *low rider*; a social misfit understood neither within his own culture nor within the Western Anglo-Saxon world to which he could not relate. For that type of individual, there was no way out. His locura was with him from the beginning to the end. *Por Vida*. For those who didn't and for those who did persevere, who did not buy in or sell out, *sangre joven y veteranos igual que no dejaron cae la bandera*, who lived through *la vida loca* and came out laughing, grabbing at life's sweet hustle, for the honor and glory of not caring to know any other way, it is in their own *locura* and from their own perspective that the Lowrider story should also be told.

En Tu Memoria

el Leonard
no le caiva que lo llamaran Lenny
sandy blonde raspy voice
green eyes toward the distant
crazy
walking out of the Allsup's in Mora
unbuttoned shirt and a quart of vodka
stuffed in his jeans
¡watcha lo que traigo aqui!
he said, as we drove away
¡que jodido, huero!
¿que no tienes miedo que te
tuersan?
he chuckled, popped the bottle open
¡ponle! he said

¡ay, que Lenny!
nomas los recuerdos quedan
aqui te va
un buen pajuelaso en tu memoria

Theirs is an endearing language of colloquialisms, pachuquisms, regional dialects, and a car-culture vocabulary as colorful as a trunk-hood mural and as vibrant as the memories they've painted and etched across our own everyday palettes of blandness and conformity.

El Chapulin y El Bionic

me topé con el Chapulin y el Bionic
en un Swap-Meet en Alburque'

pura ojelata vieja, tu sabes
y hay se comenzo el tripe

how much did you say?

Fifty

I'll take that one and one of these
and two of those
yeah, one and one of these
one of those and how much for one of these?
o.k. do I get one of those for free
you know, as a bonus for two of those
one of these and one of those?

well, that'll be seventy-eight

I thought you said forty-five?

forty-five? One of those alone is forty-five
give me seventy-five

I'll give you seventy
no, seventy-five

Bionic stands in the hot sun
wisps of hair from his pony tail
cling to his sweating forehead

¡y, wachate este, que locote!
¿que tanto? *Ten. Ten? Ten*
bueno, save it for me

that's a head lamp ring from a '37, no? *Yup*

Cool! hay vengo por el later

How Can I Tell You, Baby?

Well, Magdalena, I hope your interest hasn't begun to wane by now. This whole Low-rider thing, it's actually a multilayered phenomenon. How can one begin to describe or explain something that is so big and so small, so deep and so shallow, so high and so low, that it practically defies formal definition? I mean, could a definition such as this suffice?

Lowrider (ló'ri'dah)

1. A car culture lifestyle with its origins in California. 2. An individual whose personal identity is manifested through his automobile. 3. A car, truck, or bicycle that has been modified to achieve a lowered profile.

And even if a definitive description could be applied to illustrate the aesthetic qualities and physical characteristics of the Lowrider, there are still other insights that can be presented with underlying social, cultural, and psychological parallels. It's been proclaimed that New Mexico's cultural landscape has changed more dramatically within the last thirty years than in the previous four hundred. For the Lowrider *del norte de Nuevo Mejico*, whose daily life revolved around a direct ancestral lineage and tradition linked to *la santa fe, madre, familia, tierra y agua, cosas nuestras y sagradas*, a nurturing unconscious manifestation of spiritual sustenance formed a shield against the eminent winds of change and strengthened that inherent will of perseverance. Social commentaries and observations, equally humorous and ironic in their perspective, were interwoven into the riff-raffing, bullshittin', teasing dialogues and oral story reverberations *de platica y carilla*.

Wheels

how can I tell you
baby, oh honey, you'll
never know the ride
the ride of a lowered Chevy

slithering through the
blue dotted night along
Riverside Drive Española

poetry rides the wings
of a '59 Impala
yes, it does
and it points
chrome antennae towards

'Burque stations rocking
oldies Van Morrison
brown eyed girls
Creedence and a
bad moon rising
over Chimayo

and I guess
it also rides
on muddy Subaru's
tuned into new-age radio
on the frigid road
to Taos on weekend
ski trips

yes, baby
you and I are two
kinds of wheels
on the same road

listen, listen
to the lonesome humming
of the tracks we leave
behind

Wonderin' where I went wrong going right
And how descriptive or accurate could a portrayal of the Lowrider be without exemplifying the linguistic orations of a slow-riding, time-stealing story? Are you still with me, Magdalena, *¿Tiraremos otra vuelta?* Bueno, sit back, turn up the jams and enjoy the ride.

Easynights and a Pack of Frajos

Rosendo used to ride the buses
scoring phone numbers from *rucas*
he met at the *parque* or
along Central's bus stops and diners

three to five numbers a day, homes!
he'd say, *by the end of the week*
I know I'll get lucky with
at least one, 'ey

maybe she'll have her own canton
and I'll drop by with a bottle of wine
and some good smoke
¡y vamonos recio, carnal!

and he'd laugh, tilting his head back
taking a long drag from a Camel regular
and then he'd look at me
and laugh again, saying
¡eee, este vato!
sometimes, I just don't know
about you, bro

one night I was down at Jack's shooting pool
when the bartender yelled out
that there was a phone call
for someone whose name sounded like mine
and I was real surprised
that it was for me, you know

well, it was this fine babe from the Westside
that I'd met a few weeks before
she said that my roommate
had told her I'd be there
she said she'd been wondering
what I'd been doing
and how come I hadn't called
she wanted me to go over
I said, "great! I want to shoot a few more
games of pool, but I'll be there in a while."

not that I was really interested
in pool anymore
but, hey I couldn't let on
like I didn't ever get
those kinda calls, you know
not like those *vatos* down at Tito's
with tattoos and dead-aim stares did
leaning back against the wall
flirting with some *ruca* over the phone
laughing and teasing while the jukebox
plays Sam Cooke and me sitting there
watching and wondering where I
went wrong going right

I asked her if there was anything
she wanted me to bring over
some wine, maybe
and she said, *yeah*
that sounds good!
and could you bring some cigarettes too?

so there I was, going down the street
being all *truchas* for the *jura*
cause I didn't want nothin'
to ruin this *movida*, you know
well, I pulled into the Casa Grande
and asked for a bottle of Easynights
and a pack of *frajos*
and I sat looking through the drive-up window
at the naked pinup girls on the wall

and I started thinking of home, so far away
and how oftentimes I had nowhere to go
wishing I knew some nice girl
I could drop by to visit
and watch a mono with
or just to sit and talk to

it was a rainy night
a beautiful rainy night
and the streets were all black and wet

neon lights reflecting off of everything
and running down the street
in streams of color

and I thought of Rosendo
and how he was going to laugh
and I knew he was going to want
to know everything
¿órale, serio?
chale, you're jiving, homes

¡no, serio
her name's Carmela!

serio, homes?

yeah!

no?

¡yeah, deveras!

¡iii, este vato!
then I saw myself in the mirror
and I started laughing

sometimes, I just don't know
about you, bro

And no matter how many the years, how far removed, or how long the distance from the road once traveled, what it is still is, because it was, because we were, because we still are, at heart, cruisers cruising through the homeland. So no matter how much things change, that which gave us life, sustained us, will always be with us, here, aqui- en el pecho, en el corazon!
"Take a little trip, take a little trip, take a little trip with me."
—"Low Rider," War.

One Last Cruise:
Taos Plaza

this morning I decided
to throw one more cruise
through the plaza

en memoria de primo Bill
y de los resolaneros de aquellos tiempos

those men who had found their circle
come together
in the presence of
each other

like everything else around here
it seems all is become memory

some Saturday mornings
my father would make the 20 mile trip
into town

we'd park at the Cantu Furniture
parking lot that sits atop
the old 7-11 building
off Paseo del Pueblo Sur

it was exciting for me then
as a small boy
to know that our car
was moving across the roof
of the store below

and now, I still find it amusing,
how did that sort of engineering feat
arrive in Taos?

the other evening
I pulled into that same parking lot
and for a brief moment
contemplated leaving my truck there,
but for the sign that read

Customer Parking Only
All Others Towed Away!

this morning
as I cruised into the plaza
I saw one lone, recognizable,
living, remnant, figure
standing in faded jeans
white t-shirt, Converse canvas All Stars
and a bundle of newspapers
strapped around his shoulder

it was *el Paulie*
flat-topped, square-jawed
and looking 30 years ago
still the same

but, where were you *primo Bill?*

the park benches deserted
the covered portals no longer bursting
with children clinging to their mother's shopping stride

mama's strolling elegant
black hair curled
red lip-stick
the purse and coat
was it that Jackie Kennedy period
or was it Connie Francis?

I look out at the *parque*
los callejoncitos, las sombritas

¡nada!
¿qué paso con la palomia,
con los Indios envueltos en sus frezadas?

¿qué paso con la mini-falda?

I reach for the radio knob
and I crank up Santana
I let the sound of the timbales
snap
against
the vacant hollowness of memory
against the plaza's deserted facade
against the songbird's mournful eulogy

I notice a group of tourists
congregating next to where the old Army Surplus
used to be

I look
don't look
I look again

they pretend not to

I know I'm on trial

I let off the gas pedal
and cruise in slowly

I lean back
into the seat, lowdown
and make myself comfortable
controlling the steering wheel

with one finger here's one for the ol' times, baby!

¡dale huelo!

I remember cruising through the plaza
as a teenager with the Luna brothers, Pedro and Rupert

I remember Rupert
bad-ass *Califa's loco*
coming out to spend time with his grandparents
whenever he was wanted by the law back in Madera
I remember him
leaning far back into the seat of that black '67 chevy
sporting spit-shined *calcos* with one leg up on the dashboard
and finger-snappin' time to War tunes on the 8-track stereo

his *locura*, cocky and loud
estilo California, nothin' like *Nuevo's*
quiet and proud
back then *Taosie* wasn't a lowriding town
chale, low Impalas came from *Espa'*
I remember Rupert blurting out the window
to some *Taoseño* dudes staring us out

*"whatcha lookin' at, ese
we're just lowriding!"*

well, I remember those times
being mostly like that

the predictable unknown, lurking
waiting around like some badass dude

leaning back with one bent leg up against the wall

and somehow we'd slip through each incident
acting like it hadn't mattered whether we would or not

this morning
the people hanging out
by the coffee shop
laugh and languish

their carefree tourist manner void of history, of memory
neither attachment nor sentiment to time and place
no scars as enduring testaments
to the questions posed, the answers given
a young girl stretches out
against the oncoming morning
her breasts
her form
that figure

¡mmm, gringa!

what am I thinking?

I'm the writing instructor
of this summer's poetry class!

I can't think
act
look
this way

but hell,
I pull my shoulder back
turn my head
and stare

mmm, baby, baby!

at the stop light
a young *vato*
long hair
and a pony tail

looks at me
catches
the riff

he knows the *movida*

a tight smile forms across his mouth

Oye Como Va
Mi Ritmo

¡bongo, boom, da!
Mi Ritmo!
tsssssssssss_____ !!

for you, *carnal!*

one last cruise
around the plaza

What does all this all mean?
And because you've asked me for my insights and contributions, Magdalena, I've
tried. Though really, what can I offer you but this? Broken-tongue stories, some
thoughts, a few poems, a low-down cruise with a panoramic view into a seemingly
ominous future and a reconciliation born out of a come-what-may resiliency— *¡y que
venga lo que venga!*

Maybe you can find a way to break it all up, fragment it, present it in a more pre-
sentable way, wring out the blood, harness the spirit, translate the non-translatable,
remove the music from the song, raise the ride back up and still call it low. *Que te vaya
bien.* I couldn't do it even if I knew how. *Es todo—un viaje por mi Lowcura, por mi
Tierra Sagrada.*

New and Rejected Works
I watched a dropped
metallic lavender colored '66 Lemans
pulling out of the AutoZone onto Sunset
sporting 5/60's, Cragars, curb feelers, and rabbit ears

rabbit ears?

simón, a true period piece, *ese!*

a mid-seventies testament
a real gem of the Sunday afternoon cruise
an Ichi Coo Park, everyone's-eyes-on-it
carwash bitchin'
piece-of-ass scoring *ranfla*

what does all this all mean?

what true literary aficionado
could understand or bare even the slightest interest
in this ghost-patterned paint, chrome and rubber observation?

will this poem
be allowed to exist
alongside other genres of poetry?

to say the least of its highly improbable publication possibilities
in reputable, established "American" literary journals
that hold, in their editorial exercising power
the ability to affirm and measure
a writer's worthwhile poetic existence
no, probably not

yet, that bumper scraping cruiser
dressed in accessories from a past era
and cruising down the street literally naked
to the general public mind
was nothing but *pura poesia* to me

a statement of personal taste
much as others' interest akin to stamp collecting,
gun and knife shows or extravagant doll exhibits

as well as, say, literary journal subscriptions
for those who must have their poetic fix
mailed to them every month,
curbing an appetite for the compositional qualities
and technical structuring of a language
that works best with a certain degree of abstraction

is this poem abstract enough?

does it carry a central theme engaging a universal dialogue?
is it Eastern enough to satisfy the taste of the self-absorbent
intellectually sophisticated Western palette?

will the U.S. poet laureate nod his head in approval
and suggest that it at least be considered
placed next to the greatest poems ever written
about cats curled up on a window sill?

hmmm, maybe it's a little bit too literal
too barrio, too East LAish
or just too Aztlanish

there are, of course, some great literary enthusiasts
that could easily decipher the blue-dot
'67 Cougar taillight blinking like
a Christmas tree *carucha*,
with the boogie-woogie *rolas*
riffing out've a set of organ pipes,
and a dashboard saint protecting us
from that which does not understand us,
chain steering-wheel chariot
with the red lights flashing in the mirror

red lights flashing in the mirror?
maybe it's the poetry police!
¡ponte truchas, carnal!

great literary enthusiasts who can't even read
who do not have subscriptions to anything of self-interest
because nothing they were ever given to read
made sense to them either

great literary enthusiasts holed up in a lock-up facility
who sit waiting for their final sentence to be read to them
who without explanation or implication are told
we are simply following due process

whose hearts and souls and spirits and lives
have been censored by mainstream off-the-shelf everything
and who were given instead the concrete void of insulin
metrazol electricity
hydrotherapy, psychotherapy
pingpong & amnesia

Levi's car. Photo courtesy of Levi Romero.

oops, now, how did that get in there?
how come nothing in the great american poetry anthology
reads like the america I know?
or sounds like the chrome tipped
cherry-bombed idle of a lowered *bomba* at the stop light
with a tattered page manuscript
lying under a pile of sorry assed
thank you for your interest
rejection letters carpeting the floor?

Note: "Lowcura: An Introspective *Virtual Cruise* through an American Subcultural Tradition" first appeared as a section in *A Poetry of Remembrance: New and Rejected Works* (UNM Press 2008).

13

In the Center and on the Edge at Once

RINA SWENTZELL

SATURDAY AFTERNOON, JULY 23, 1960, HIGHLANDS UNIVERSITY campus in the northern New Mexico town of Las Vegas was quiet. A few students were at study tables scattered in the reading room of the Rogers Library. I was tending the special collections desk. A tall Anglo student came up to the counter and, with rather thick fingers, pointed at a book request slip he placed in front of me. When I returned with the book, he took it without a word and walked off. I looked at his slender back, long legs in khaki pants, and thin arms in a short-sleeved shirt. I fumbled out of my cubicle and followed to retrieve the book. I tapped his high shoulder with my left hand and held out the other one with open palm and summoning fingers while I whispered, "You must sign it out." He sighed, nodding his head. After the library closed, he was walking along the railroad tracks at the same time and in the same direction as my two Navajo girlfriends and I. He talked with great interest to one of them. However, two weeks later, after the morning service at the Taos Baptist Indian Mission, where my father preached hell and damnation, Ralph and I married. My father did not want us to marry, but he did get a pastor friend to do the ceremony.

My parent's family of eight children had moved from Santa Clara Pueblo to Taos in 1959 so that our father could serve as pastor of the Baptist Mission for Taos Pueblo people. During our strange fifteen or so years in Taos, our father acted like a southern Baptist minister but was really just himself: an independent thinker and a person very capable of being whatever he wanted to be at any time. He was a shoemaker, paid baseball pitcher, farmworker, farmer, builder, carpenter, electrician, mechanic, fisherman, hunter, Baptist preacher, womanizer, and alcoholic in any order he chose. His parents died when he was five years old in the 1916 influenza epidemic. Except for a few years at St. Catherine Indian School in Santa Fe, from which he ran away at the age of twelve, he quickly learned self-sufficiency and personal capability. Later, when he returned to the pueblo, he did not easily honor communal living and obligations. One day, the Santa Clara tribal council came to our house to throw out two women

Rina Swentzell, 2010. Photo by Jack Loeffler.

Baptist missionaries whom our mother had befriended. My father simply stood in their path with a gun and they withdrew. That action obligated him to a relationship with the two missionaries and eventually the Baptist Church. However, he did not become a Christian in the usual sense. He wanted the outdoors, the mountains, the streams, and soil. He wanted what he could touch and feel, so he preached suffering and hell. Love and God were abstractions. For him paradoxes were not an issue. Light and love were minor next to fire in hell. Fire and suffering were real.

My mother grew up in a still traditionally strong Santa Clara Pueblo, where sky, mountains, and hills defined centers of relationships with wind, sun, plants, and animals. Human living focused on respect for all those relationships that defined life itself. Although she joined my father during his active years of involvement in Christian practices, she firmly held on to the Pueblo values of relatedness, respect, caretaking, harmony, equality, and sharing of resources and property. Interestingly, our years in Taos coincided with the numerous Taos communes of young Anglo people from across the country seeking these same values. They dreamed of egalitarian, nonpatriarchal, nonauthoritarian communities in tune with nature. They were a generation hungry for peace, kindness, sharing—and escape from war mongering. The Vietnam War was vibrating in every American home with a television. Taos, with its expansive vistas of mountains, sagebrush plains, and hot springs, drew thousands of spiritually and physically hungry young dissidents. It was literally an invasion, some coming to live there and others just passing through. Instant communities, communes, were formed.

With vibrantly colored clothes, long hair, and bandannas, the hippies were everywhere. The Pueblo people's way of life resonated for them. Our family and the people of Taos Pueblo mostly observed with keen interest. But some interacted with the hippies—in their communes, but not within the pueblo. Little Joe Gomez, a friend of my father, served as spiritual guide and teacher for peyote ceremonies in a few communes. For the most part, the townspeople, Hispanics and Anglos, reacted with less tolerance. Town meetings were held to address "the hippie problem." Townspeople felt assaulted, angry, and fearful that their town was being despoiled and their lands devalued or settled on. Reaction was intense. There were a few bombings of hippie buses and burnings of hippie houses. The air seemed full of fear and anger, as well as the hope and dreams of a loving world.

After marriage, Ralph and I lived as students in Las Vegas, over the mountains from Taos. Except for the lively art department on campus, Las Vegas and the rest of the university seemed removed from what was happening in Taos during the 1960s and '70s. People seemed unaware of stirrings about the Vietnam War, capitalism, and consumerism. It was, and still is, very different from towns in the Rio Grande valley. Jerry West, a fellow art student at Highlands and now a celebrated Santa Fe artist, writes: "I have had a long love affair with Las Vegas, New Mexico. I like the color and character of the town, which was a railroad town in decline after World War II. It never became much of a tourist town, and it still struggles with its deep roots of cultural conflict that remain, however, part of the vibrant energy of the place" (West, p. 93).

Las Vegas was the entry point from the east into the greater Southwest. There is the Old Town of pre-railroad days with adobe mud houses around a plaza, and there

Left: *Little Joe Gomez, Taos peyote roadman at New Buffalo during construction, 1970s. Photo by Seth Roffman. *Right: *Little Joe Gomez's home near Taos. Photo by Seth Roffman.*

is New Town with numbered linear streets and lumber-framed Victorian and Queen Anne–style, many-storied houses with widow's walks on the roofs to watch for incoming ships bringing in loved ones. Strange, but intriguing. There were no ships coming in, but there was the train puffing over the grassy midwestern prairie bringing in milled lumber, glass panes, and all the other accoutrements of American/European life. In the summer of 1899, Theodore Roosevelt rode in for a Rough Riders Reunion. And in the summer of 1960, Ralph rode in from Chanute Air Force Base in Illinois, where he had served a four-year term—playing the clarinet in the band. He was really an antiwar thinker who struggled against the authoritative and unreasonable disciplinary tactics of the government war institutions. He did not enlist to be patriotic.

Ralph, like the young people invading Taos during the same time, was running from the East Coast. He wanted distance from factory-smoke-covered Paterson, New Jersey. He wanted freedom from what he saw as a repressive, profit-making economic system and society based on Christian morality of absolute rights and wrongs. Even the weather, he felt, was depressive, clammy and grey. Here in the Southwest, the expansive blue skies, exhilarating mountain views, clean air, and real Indians were life altering, as they were for the young hippies in Taos. Indians had been a fascination for Ralph since childhood. The day after we married, he sent off a postcard to his parents letting them know that he had just married a Pueblo Indian girl. His parents went to the encyclopedia. They found an Acoma Pueblo woman with a pot on her head and were relieved. "She looks more civilized than the other Indians," they replied. On my side, some relatives were verbal about my marrying a "medicana" (Tewa version of the Spanish word for American) and diluting my Pueblo blood and heritage. For Ralph and me, Las Vegas was an excellent cultural middle place.

During our first years in Las Vegas, we took care of one of the large Victorian houses in New Town with four rental apartments for a woman from Grants, New Mexico, who showed up every couple of months for the rent money that we collected and assurance that we had cleaned, maintained, and repaired the house in exchange for our $45 per month apartment. We had no family wealth. We struggled on my Bureau of Indian Affairs scholarship and $15 a week from Ralph's father. Ralph's retired parents had been factory workers in the silk mills of East Paterson, and the money they sent was a considerable amount for them and us. Life as students suited us both. We met like-minded people interested in philosophical ideas, social and economic justice, and artistic expression. The gathering place on campus was the art department, which stayed opened all night, highly unusual for any institution. Jerry West claims that his work with artists on campus at that time created a profound personal transformation in him. We were affected as well. It was no commune, but it offered interest, interaction, and friends for a lifetime.

To visit family in Taos, we caught rides with my brother, who became a close friend to Ralph. Sometimes, my father would generously loan us a car, knowing that Ralph could not drive. Mostly I drove, but eventually Ralph could do the dangerous, snow-covered mountain road from Las Vegas to Taos. One spring break, we ventured farther. We caught a bus to Cortez, Colorado, and hitched a ride to Mesa Verde. It was a major adventure for me to visit that particular ancestral site. We had enough money to stay one night on the mesa in a small cabin but not enough to feed our one-year-old daughter on the bus trip back to Las Vegas. That trip planted a seed that blossomed into later wanderings similar to what the hippies were doing in the 1960s.

Although Ralph was a psychology and science major, our friends were artists and Ralph was a musician. However, unusually for that period in the 1960s, drugs did not become a part of our lives. Ralph and friends experimented with mushrooms and peyote, but their experiences didn't seem to excite enough interest to hold them. It didn't occur to me to try them. Life was stimulating. Music, jazz and the blues, which Ralph introduced to me, were mind blowing. There were no such sounds in the Pueblo world. Deep drumbeats holding and reminding us of our place within this earth were simple next to the excitable sounds of the Beatles or the phrasing of Frank Sinatra or the almost whining voice of counterculturalist Joan Baez. I especially liked her recording of one of Bob Dylan's early songs, "With God On Our Side."

Life moved on, and we went off to the University of Minnesota. Ralph was accepted into their graduate psychology program for a doctorate. I taught first graders in a typical American elementary school in Minneapolis. We were absolutely miserable. It all felt too sanitized, standardized, and institutionalized. After three months, we both gave up trying to fit into an educational system that was still modeled after the industrial revolution and factory mentality of production—step-by-step output of good, upright citizens. Ralph was offered a position with 3M as a computer programmer. The money was stunning and a three-bedroom house in a suburban neighborhood was included. We looked at the house on a corner lot and decided to pack our bags and our two little girls into an old Chevrolet Corvair with a hole in its floor. We headed back to Las Vegas, New Mexico.

Our second term in Las Vegas was different. Ralph was taken on as a computer and research assistant in the psychology department of Highlands University with a modest salary. Old friends had moved on. New friends were older, established professional people with respectable houses in New Town. We could afford a small bungalow house between a funeral home and an abandoned four-story Queen Anne mansion. I returned to the art department to experiment with stoneware pottery, using commercial clays fired in high-temperature kilns. Santa Clara Pueblo's long tradition of pottery making used local clays, outdoor pit fires, and low temperatures.

Rina Swentzell. Photos courtesy of Athena Steen.

A merging of the two traditions happened as my girls and I scoured arroyos and hills for clay sources that would tolerate high temperatures. I was ecstatic taking clays traditionally used by Santa Clara Pueblo people to achieve mottled earth-colored, high-fired glazes. Roaming nearby places set in a yearning to see farther and farther beyond the next hill. Strangely, the elitist, and in my opinion conservative, St. John's College in Santa Fe, which taught the art of liberal thinking through the great books of the Western world, provided that possibility.

On the evening of labor pains for our third daughter, Poem, who was given that typical 1960s name by her father, Ralph was hired at St. John's College. He was hired for his science background and, mostly, for his love of thinking and discussion. He discussed the great books of the Western world enthusiastically for nine months of the year, but each summer for eight years we roamed the country in revamped Volkswagen buses. We drove through five engines in two buses. Ralph built bunk beds for the three girls and saved room in the back for our bed. We rented our modest house on the west side of Santa Fe to opera people for the entire summer. Two of those summers were in Santa Clara Canyon, where we lived alongside the stream, fishing, building a tipi and an outdoor cooking oven, baking bread and pies, taking day-long hikes, and singing along with Ralph on his guitar in the evenings. We discovered

ancient Pueblo ruins dating to the time when the old people walked hundreds of miles into the Rio Grande region and onto the Pajarito Plateau from the Mesa Verde area during the late twelfth and thirteenth centuries. Those sites in my childhood backyard spurred my intense and lifelong interest in Pueblo architecture as an expression of its philosophical tradition. That tradition, I was to learn, held ideas that some physicists and some Eastern and Western philosophers, as well as the hippie freedom lovers, were espousing in the 1960s.

Other summers we crisscrossed the United States and Canada in our Volkswagen bus, never staying in motels or cities. We wanted the calm and beauty of the outdoors, much like the young invaders of the Taos sage plains. We followed dirt roads to their end, especially in the Southwest, and parked for days where they stopped on the edge of a canyon or in the middle of nowhere. If we had any destination, it was any national park. One morning, after a late-night arrival on a random dirt road we had taken, we found ourselves on the firing range of a military base near the lower Colorado River. Weeks later, we visited for hours with a French man walking and pulling his coffin on wheels through the wilds of Canada. He was old and was prepared for the inevitable. The East Coast was always stressful. We did not do well in heavy traffic, and dirt roads to nowhere were hard to find. Visits to Ralph's family never lasted more than four days before our yearning for home, blue skies, and clear air drove us again into the Southwest.

On two special trips to Denver and later to California, we visited my younger brother. He had just returned from the Vietnam War, where a hand grenade exploded as he was throwing it back into the jungle at whoever threw it at him and his unit. Blinded and disabled with a shattered right hand, he was hospitalized for months in Denver and then was sent to California to learn to move about with a seeing-eye dog. Visiting the Denver hospital was surreal. The walls were white, the bed stands were white, the bed coverings were white, the bandages on legs, arms, and heads were white. Michael's bed was at the far end of the long corridor lined with white beds on both sides. He did not know we were coming. I gently ran my fingers down his left hand, which was molding a lump of clay on his nightstand. He had asked the staff for clay to start sculpting memories. Slowly he turned his bandaged head and asked, "Who is it?"

A year later, we walked with him and his seeing-eye dog around the Palo Alto, California, hospital block. He was always a happy, calm person, but there was, after Vietnam, a peculiar gentleness in the way he walked, moved, and reached out to feel the world. Sitting on a grassy area by the hospital, I asked if he was angry about not being able to see. Was he angry about the war? After a long pause and in a voice so quiet that I could hardly hear against the noise of the traffic, he whispered, "No." There was no more; it was simply "No." I was red angry at the senseless war and his painful situation; how could he not be? Periodically, through the years, I have asked him the same question, and he still admits no anger but does add that blindness gives him a kind of life and vision that eyes do not. Today, with his left hand, he sculpts memories of fishing, hunting, living in Santa Clara Pueblo, and even times in Vietnam. But he also continues to suffer intense headaches that keep him in bed for many days of any week. His entire body, including his spinal cord, was pierced by shrapnel from the hand grenade. Government and public doctors across the country have failed to mend the spinal fluid leakage and cord damage.

After our visit with Michael in Palo Alto, we went, with purpose, to the Haight-Ashbury district of San Francisco, where we heard hippies were actively protesting the Vietnam War. The Taos invasion of hippies was minor compared with the numbers of young people who sat, walked, sang, and smoked in the San Francisco streets and parks. These were impressive gatherings of people striving for a voice and place in their country and world. How did they eat? Where did they live? How did their groupings work? Where was this dream of a better society filled with love and care coming from? Could peace really replace war? Even with such questioning, there was an air of hope and excitement that something within our universal human consciousness was once again stirring and strengthening. We drove through the district wondering at them and at ourselves. We drove out of that city and its harried traffic, which seemed mostly oblivious to dreams of peace, love, and hope. We drove through the night to Joshua Tree National Park, near the Mexican border. It was great to be once again where rocks and trees thrived in their natural, native place.

Ralph and I acknowledged our shared dreams and desires with the Taos and San Francisco freedom seekers but did not quite realize the contradictions that shaped our lives and still do. We all traveled in buses and cars fueled by gasoline products of the consumptive society that we disliked and kicked against. We needed the financial security of institutions (like St. John's or wealthy parents) to afford our own consumptive roaming. Did any people before recent times have such easy and fast transportation? Instant communities of the hippies were hard to maintain and sustain because rootedness in place is long term. Sustainability takes intimate knowledge of soil, water, and wind. Life in fast motion and short-term commitment to any place are pure consumption. We were all tourists, in effect. And we do change and affect any environment with our simple presence. Those hippies and other newcomers wanting pure air, direct communication with nature, and simplicity of life helped change that which they desired. Yet we keep moving fast and easy, without commitment to place. On the other hand, change and movement are embedded in life itself. Life is one paradox after another, and we somehow manage to continue.

Shortly after our wanderings, Ralph and I became part-time homesteaders on an arid mesa near Madrid, New Mexico. Tarantulas, rattlesnakes, and coyotes kept us company. The groundwater in the Madrid region had been poisoned during the early-twentieth-century rush to extract coal, gold, turquoise, and silver, so we carried drinking water but did eventually set up a rainwater collection system. Immense skies and distant views of the Jemez Mountains provided energy to build two simple shelters with hand tools: screwdriver, hammer, and handsaw. We had no electricity or any other utilities.

During our intense personal back-to-earth effort, Ralph died in 2005. The influence of the 1960s era remained with us throughout our marriage. And today I still visit the mesa and feel its stark beauty, marvel at billowing clouds, and get lost in the jeweled night sky. Its quietness, dryness, and expansiveness are like the sage plains of Taos. As with that specific Taos landscape, human population on the mile-long Madrid mesa has increased. There are now five houses instead of the two of thirty-five years ago. Not only did Ralph and I add to the human population, we helped change the character of the mesa. A once pristine mesa top now has roads going off in all directions for our four-wheel vehicles and fences, showing our rabid obsession with owning land. Every corner of the earth is now traveled and possessed. Movement and change. Maybe it is as Edward Abbey said in 1982: "The reason so many people are fleeing the cities at every opportunity to go tramping into the wilds is that wilderness offers a taste of adventure, a chance for the rediscovery of our ancient, preagricultural, preindustrial freedom. This elemental impulse still survives in our blood, nerves, dreams, and desires, suppressed but not destroyed by the mere five thousand years of agricultural serfdom, a mere two hundred years of industrial peonage, which culture has attempted to impose on what evolution designed as a feeling, thinking, liberty-loving animal" (Abbey, p. 120).

We are, I agree, mostly liberty loving. Some of us continue to hope for peace and love on this beautiful planet, and that hope arises in small and large waves throughout human history—like the wave of the 1960s. And there are always others who act otherwise. The contradictions built into our world seem to ensure continual movement and change; it seems that we do live somewhere between possibility and reality. Yet somehow things happen—somehow from faraway places, people can come together—like on the sage plains of Taos, or at the end of a dirt road, or in a college library on a quiet Saturday afternoon.

Sources

Abbey, Edward. *Down the River*. New York: Dutton, 1982.

West, Jerry R. *Jerry West: The Alchemy of Memory*. Santa Fe: Museum of New Mexico Press, 2015.

Rina Swentzell. Photo courtesy of Athena Steen.

14

Indian Tales

JACK LOEFFLER

FIVE CENTURIES OF CONTACT with Europeans and their descendants have been hard on the indigenous peoples of the Americas. Genocide, slavery, religious persecution, dislocation from culture, dislocation from homeland, and devastation of sacred habitat are some of the ways Indian people have been treated from the Atlantic to the Pacific. And yet Indians of different homelands and habitats continue to live within their traditions in spite of a half-millennium of abuse from the sons and daughters of Europe. By continuing to survive, the Indian peoples remain America's first counterculturalists.

The Southwest is the most arid part of North America. It is also homeland to numerous Native cultures, including Pueblo, Hopi, Ute, Navajo, Apache, O'odham, Mojave, Yuman, Yaqui, and Havasupai. Other cultures have disappeared. Those who have remained true to their cultural traditions have displayed tremendous endurance. Navajo artist Shonto Begay tells of life in the Bureau of Indian Affairs (BIA) boarding school that he was forced to attend during the early 1960s.

> Yeah, I went to Shonto to the boarding school. It was . . . about five miles from my home, my sheep camp. But it was across the canyon over a mesa. It might as well have been on the other side of the world, because we're not allowed to see our parents, we're not allowed to go home, we're not allowed to speak our language, we're not allowed to worship our way. We were just totally repressed at every turn. And this was in the days when religion was eked out to young Navajo boys, young Navajo kids—I guess all Native kids. Religion at the time was being eked out pretty much by your height. Three lines were scratched on the wall. If you were below the lowest line and shorter, you were Catholic. If you were above the tallest lines, that meant you were the tallest. You were Mormons. The ones in between were Presbyterians. They would set the lines for girls so there was an equal mixture. So

Artist Shonto Begay painting. Photo by Jack Loeffler.

Shonto Begay, The Black Mesa Ceremony. Photo by Tom Alexander Photography.

I had no idea why I was a Catholic the first year, and Catholicism was interesting. I don't remember learning anything, but I remember being amused by this friar in black walking around and it was just interesting. It was very foreign again.

I took it all in as a curiosity. Every year, of course, you would rotate it, so if you were Catholic last year, you were Presbyterian this year. Then next year you were Mormon. I remember every Monday was specially set aside just for religious Christian indoctrination all day long. Some were entertaining, some weren't. But after a while you just kind of judged the religion by how much they gave at Christmas time, and Mormons were very generous, so everybody wanted to be Mormons around Christmas time. I guess it was good that they mixed it all up and rotated us, because it just made it very interesting and not so sacred. It was something different.

Mine [religion] remains unquestionably, *unquestionably*, alone and very sacred to me without any deviation. It seemed like between all these other three major religions there were—I was just a ball of confusion. By the time summer comes around, you're free of the boarding school tethers. You kick your shoes off, and I guess you take the best of what you learned from all these religions. At least I did. You take the best of what you learned and disregard the others. So that's how I was brought up and raised. Of course, we held on to the tradition of the elders. In the summertime we just immersed ourselves back in the beauty of the Beauty Way and Blessing Way and the Enemy Way Ceremonies. I knew the songs, I knew the chants, and partook in the Star-Gazing Ceremony of the diagnostician and all the ways. I Ierded sheep, heard the thunderstorm, was buffeted by the blazing sun and the wind. It was a joy.

But living in two worlds, it was totally a schizophrenic childhood.

But boarding school was so horrendous, very horrendous, that I think about it in amazement because thirteen boys that grew up very close from here with the boarding school ever since I was a little kid . . . [there are] only three of us alive. It's a lot of casualty to the brutality of boarding school.

Shonto Begay was born in that part of the Colorado Plateau between Black Mesa and the tiny community of Shonto south of Navajo Mountain. This remains a region where Navajo traditions are still practiced with commitment to the mythic process.

A few hundred miles to the south in the Sonoran Desert is the homeland of the Tohono O'odham, formerly known as the Papago Indians. The Sonoran Desert is the most luxuriant of the four North American deserts and has a long history of human

Camillus Lopez, Tohono O'odham elder. Photo by Jack Loeffler.

habitation. Camillus Lopez is a lore master and a great defender of O'odham tradition. He has attended the white man's schools but now devotes his life to documenting the old ways that have sustained his people for generations. He recognizes the intrinsic value of the mythic process through which indigenous cultures intuitively define their relationship to homeland.

You mimic the movements of nature. In O'odham there's no categorizing, no science, no math, no foreign language. Everything is the same, so when you go to a person, you go to them with the whole of everything. If you go there for a reason, to talk to somebody for this reason, you're bringing everything else.

I noticed that in O'odham culture everything is cold or hot or dark or light or whatever. But in the Western culture there's a lot of numbers and degrees and miles and those things. When in O'odham something's far, then it's far. If it's cold, it's cold. Because I hear a lot of times with westerners that I work with, they talk like if it's cloudy, they'll say something like, "Oh, this is strange weather for June." In O'odham if that's the way it wants to be, then go with it. So everything's based on the outside because it's affecting the inside. When you live as part of an environment, I guess you become it, and everybody else around you is it.

In O'odham long before, you weren't walking through the desert to take a walk. You didn't walk through the desert to go from here to there. You actually were meeting all these trees. So it's actually like a high reverence where you could stop and pick a berry or whatever from a tree and at the same time you're talking to the tree, saying you've been standing here and these are good for me and I'll use them right. So it's not where you're just taking a walk. But you're always remembering that things are alive and that you're not alone.

I walk through the desert. If I see a palo verde tree, I look at it and see that the leaves are yellow, they're pink, or whatever color the leaves are. Then I think that that's the time of the year in that way. So you recognize the tree as you would recognize a person walking by. Two O'odham in the middle of the desert coming together and they start talking, they're not just talking to themselves. You're being overheard by all this other stuff around you. So there's always been that kind of reverence. If you see a palo verde tree standing there and you come by, you notice it. Then it's like both people know where you're at. So it's not just singing or talking to the trees as you're walking along, but keeping in mind that you're there with them and that they're just as much alive as you are. I think trees sense more of that than humans do.

In O'odham culture, women don't necessarily go looking for power, for strength, because they have so much strength already. They have a womb where babies are made. That's a lot of power. When they go into menstruation, they used to go out and get away from men because they might make them [men] sick.

Men are always seeking power. That's why men do the vision quest. That's why men do all these things, looking for the answers for whatever, for strength. They're the ones that go to war. So it's those kind[s] of songs that can give me some kind of strength, I guess, empowerment to push. A lot of people talk about Baboquivari, where I'itoi lives, with great reverence. There's a great power there. That's true, but to me it's these mountains that are here in Santa Rosa, these mountains that I remember.

Each place has a place in the natural order. To do something with that place, just to take something out from the natural order, would cause disturbance to the rest of the order. I guess, like the river, how it kind of went into the ground because the farmers were taking from the water below and the river disappeared in Santa Cruz. That makes the water table go down. Therefore, it doesn't rain so much here because there's no natural water coming from the ground evaporating into the sky to cause the moisture that we need up there for the clouds to come through in the same way.

You build something somewhere, the respect. You have to remember that there's an order there. You go somewhere and you take a rock, you don't place the rock with anything there, you disturb the balance. That kind of a thing, you know.

The mountain holds a special place in history or time. There's a reason that it's put there. Nobody owns it, it owns itself. In O'odham, it's a strange thing to own land because the land was there for everybody. It was placed there by I'itoi to serve a purpose so people could live there and do what they needed to there. You take over and you call it yours without the respect that it should have. It was there before. When ants are living in a place and you're coming for a picnic for one day, you put out ant repellent. You destroy the ants, you destroy the natural flow. So when the ants are gone, you need to replace it with something, but you're just taking off and the ants are gone and you've only used the place for one day or for a few hours. You don't think of what's going to happen ten years from now.

This place has been here for many, many thousands of years, and human beings have only been here for ten thousand, twelve thousand years. Then in just, what, fifty years, all of a sudden all this stuff is happening. There's no regard for the land.

You try with respect to get it to the way that you found it with an attitude where it's not there for just you, but it's there for all, not just people, but for all living creatures. What you do there is going to affect everything else. What you do to the land you do to yourself, and eventually it'll catch back to you. You have an attitude that you want this place to be here with the respect that it had for all these years with the great power that it has. If you want the power, it's there, but you have to be open to it. If you're there for yourself, that's okay, but you have to remember that other people, other living creatures, are in this life with everybody else. If they can respect, it's not hard for someone else.

To learn a thing, you have to learn to respect things. If you don't respect things, it's just because you never learned it somewhere. So to those people that are there for themselves, they have to learn how to respect things. Because if they don't, it affects everybody.

Community is everything. It's the stars. It's the ground way under. It's the little ant that comes across. It's Coyote. It's the buzzard. The actions and stuff, it reflects who you are. And if you can see yourself in it, then you're there. But if you can't look at nature and see yourself in it, then you're too far away. That's why I think one of the things people need to do is go out and become, look at the mirror of nature and try to see themselves in it. Because if they can see themselves in it, then they can help themselves by helping the environment.

John Trudell was a leading Indian activist. Born on the Santee Sioux Indian Reservation in northern Nebraska in 1946, he served in the United States Navy during the early years of the Vietnam War. After he was discharged, he attended San Bernardino Valley College, where he learned the fundamentals of radio broadcasting.

In 1969, Trudell became the spokesperson for the United Indians of All Tribes' occupation of Alcatraz, where he founded Radio Free Alcatraz, which was broadcast at night over KPFA public radio in Berkeley. Here, he discussed Native American issues and played Native American music. This lasted until 1971. Then Trudell joined the American Indian Movement (AIM), and from 1973 till 1979, he served as its national chairman. Trudell's activism brought national attention to many inequities visited upon the American Indians throughout the twentieth century. In his later years, Trudell promoted the necessity for achieving a higher level of consciousness throughout American culture. John Trudell inspired a generation of activists, both Indian and non-Indian. He died of natural causes in December 2015.

Tara Evonne Trudell is John Trudell's firstborn child. Tara's mother, born in Las Vegas, New Mexico, in 1944, lived with Trudell when he attended college in San Bernardino, where Tara was born in 1968. She accompanied her parents to Alcatraz, where she lived for nearly two years. Trudell's second wife, Tina Manning, was an activist in the Duck Valley Shoshone Tribe in northeastern Nevada. Tara was close both to her mother, her stepmother, Tina, and her three stepsiblings.

I interviewed Tara Trudell in Las Vegas, New Mexico.

Top: *Tara Evonne Trudell. Photo by Jack Loeffler.* Bottom: *John Trudell. Photo courtesy of Tara Trudell.*

My father was a Vietnam veteran. He was taught that when you are in distress, one way to seek help or to let people know, you hang a flag upside down as a sign of distress. So my father, as a political statement, took a flag to, I think, the stairs of the Bureau of Indian Affairs in Washington [or the FBI building], and protested the treatment of the Indian peoples here in America [who were] being sent out to these reservations, and being sent to be assimilated into the cities, where they were losing their identity and turning to alcohol and drugs. It was a very strong political statement that he made by burning the upside-down flag as a sign of distress. Tragically and unfortunately, less than fourteen hours later, Tina [John Trudell's second wife] and her children, my brothers and sisters, and her [Tina's] mother and father were trapped in a fire on Duck Valley Reservation. She was staying with her mother and father at this time; she did that a lot when my father traveled. She smelled the smoke, she woke up, she woke up her parents, and they tried to get out of the house, but because the house burned so quickly and so aggressively— it was an act of arson—they were locked in, and they were not able to open any of the doors. Everything was sealed shut, which is bizarre and tragic. So they all died in the fire except Arthur Manning, Tina's father, who at the very end threw himself through the living-room window and suffered third-degree burns. But everybody else perished in that fire. The tribal police there in Duck Valley did a really small investigation and wrote it off as a fire that started on the back porch. My father later on had it investigated by a private investigator, who concluded that it was an act of arson.

Left: *Sign at Oraibi, Hopi Independent Nation, Arizona. 1970s. Photo by Seth Roffman.*
Right: *Sign at Big Mountain, Arizona. Photo courtesy of the Lisa Law Production Archives.*

This tragedy is one of many mysterious deaths that have befallen American Indians since the end of the Indian wars in the late nineteenth century. Nevertheless, the Red Power Movement is a powerful force in the greater counterculture movement that has affected virtually every aspect of American life since the mid-twentieth century.

In the early 1970s many Hopi and Navajo Indians joined forces to try to halt both the strip mining of Black Mesa and the pumping of water at the rate of 2,000 gallons a minute from the Pleistocene aquifer that lies beneath Black Mesa to slurry coal to a coal-fired power plant near Bullhead City, Nevada. The Navajo and Hopi homelands in northern Arizona are rich in coal, uranium, and other nonrenewable resources.

To divide and conquer the protesting Navajos and Hopis, politicians and their supporters in the coal industry revived the idea of moving some ten thousand traditional Navajos out of the area known as the Joint Use Area shared by both Hopi and Navajo people on Big Mountain. To my mind, the two main reasons for Navajo relocation were to thwart the strengthening coalition between traditional Hopis and Navajos who were rebelling against an alien governing body and to clear the way for further corporate incursions into Indian homelands. Congressman Sam Steiger (R., Arizona) and his colleagues were intent on economic growth even at the expense of traditional cultures.

Roberta Blackgoat, a Navajo born in 1917, was threatened by the program known as Navajo Relocation. It would force her to leave her homeland on Big Mountain, the southern part of Black Mesa, where Peabody Coal was scooping out the bowels of the mountain to feed coal-fired power plants that continue to pour tens of thousands of tons of carbon dioxide into the atmosphere. Mrs. Blackgoat invited me into her hogan late one afternoon in 1982 after we had herded her sheep into the corral for the night.

She allowed me to record her account of her plight and her perspective on being forced to leave the area between the four sacred mountains that define the boundaries of Dinetah, the Navajo homeland.

They really should know about the songs and the prayers. According to this, Mount Blanca, it has a lot of prayers and songs, and also Mount Taylor and San Francisco Peak and Mount Hesperus [the four sacred mountains that define the boundaries of Navajo country]. These have been left for us to use through our lives, and what our own people had been using to live a long life and what they had when they were living. They had the songs that were really sacred for them, and they've been using them for their culture and all these things, to have property and livelihood with livestock and all these things. That was the way they handled things easy, by the posts of this "hogan" [Navajo homeland] of mountains.

This executive order [for relocation] is right in the middle on the west side of the hogan, right inside here. This is where we're losing the whole area here [*sweeping her arm over the landscape*]. If we lose, where are we going to put our medicine? And a sick person should be sitting on the north side of the executive order [for relocation], and on this side would be a medicine man. Mainly this place is the big sacred spot right here, where they're going to make a sand painting if they wanted to have prayers. Where are they going to put that in the baskets? This is the main spot right here.

We can't take these baskets or medicines on either side of . . . these sacred mountains. This is a special spot . . . all these big mountains and Navajo Mountain are really sacred for the four sacred mountains. They're messengers. They sent words or news or something like that to these sacred mountains. Whatever is happening out here in these four sacred mountains, they sent words to these, when there's a medicine man that uses prayers, and then this is that area where the winds sent the message to these four main sacred mountains.

This is why we always say we hate to have these mountains to be destroyed, because it talks like us in their way. Just like the trees, when the wind, it breezes and you could hear the sounds of it. And even the grasses, the grasses or whatever the herbs are, it really makes noise. And they're talking to each other by whispering or whatever it is. They might be praying or they might be singing, it's the sound that we hear. If they're destroyed, we can't use any medicine out of it. . . . These plants . . . some are medicine, some are food, and if it's a real serious illness comes around to a person, then we use some strong herbs for it. And they're growing around among us.

Here a lot of things have been planned on this area—that's the mine [Black Mesa] or the uranium or the oil, whatever comes up—and they want to start destroying our medicines. This is the main point—that we can't give up. As long as I'm here, I'm not going to give up. According to our old ancestors, they said don't ever give up. There's something going to happen. It's going to be ruined someday, or either you're going to be shot or you're going to be destroyed first and then they're going to destroy the land. So I think it's coming up near every day. It's what we've been thinking.

My great-great-grandmother is buried on this side just a little ways wherever you've been herding sheep. And my next great-grandmother buried right across the canyon here. And my grandmother, I saw her when I was about six years old and she died. She's buried on the south side of here. Some of her children are buried here. And us grandkids, my sister and brothers, are buried around here too. And my children and also my grandchildren. So I just couldn't say I'm going to leave or I need to be relocated. I can't do it. My roots is just about that big, maybe three or four down deep, so it can't be pulled out.

Well, I'll just load up my gun and then walk out towards them if they start coming to me. I'll just tell them that I'm going to remain here as long as I live, even if they try to take me to jail or whatever.

In 2014, I interviewed my cousin, Richard Grow. An engineer with the Environmental Protection Agency in San Francisco, he has also been a hardcore activist who has worked closely with Indians to attempt to end inequities visited upon them by the US government with the support of its corporate counterparts. Richard was a close friend of Roberta Blackgoat, who frequently called on him for support at Big Mountain.

She was so warm. Our last adventure as far as the Big Mountain Support Group that I was working with was at Roberta's invitation. It was in 1989, actually, on Super Bowl Sunday, and I got a call from Danny [Blackgoat, her son]. It had to do with the bulldozers that were coming out to Big Mountain in about two weeks. Danny Blackgoat said, "My mom wants you to round up three or four people and come on down here." Before, it had always been round up a lot of people when they had these big gatherings there at Big Mountain.

After we got down there, the Indians did some ceremonies over us to get us prepared to confront the bulldozers. It all came together on the right day, and we all got indicted. There was a trial that was going to happen over the course of January, February, and into March. There was a dramatic scene in the courtroom where the Feds were getting ready, preparing their case. They took a posture: "We're sending them away for five years!"

That's interesting. How did you get into it in the first place, the Big Mountain thing?

I came from Detroit, where in the early 1970s I was still working with the radical black and white movement. Basically we thought we were going to have a revolution, though not a violent one. We were going to take over Detroit. Several years later, by 1979, I had moved out to the West Coast, to the Bay Area. I thought that I needed to give myself a year to check the scene out. Logically, I would come from Detroit and hook up with the black radical movement out here, whatever version it was. By that time, a lot of the Black Panthers had been executed. The best advice I got from black radicals in Detroit was, "Take your time, open your mind, and you'll see." I don't know what they really meant, but it was really good advice. I spent a year wandering around, and one of the places I visited was the AIM house in Oakland, the American Indian Movement house.

It turned out that the Indians were opening themselves up to white folks in a way that they hadn't so much before, kind of emulating the Black Panthers. They were looking for folks who were non-Indians, especially white folks, who understood the environmental stuff. So I think that was kind of the hook for me. I wandered into the AIM house, where they had potlucks every other week, and I'd show up for those. I was ignorant, and the first time I was going to go to the AIM house for a potluck, I started to take a jug of wine with me. I'm the old hippie, right? Fortunately somebody gave me a clue before I carried it into the AIM house. They were totally alcohol and drug free. (I learned later that that didn't include weed.)

I had some understanding but no experience. I met some hard-core urban Navajo folks who were city Indians but who were still from the Rez [Navajo Reservation]. There were Navajos over here who saw that part of their work was to educate non-Indians as to what's going on. At that point it concerned the coal mine at Burnham [New Mexico]. There were more coal-fired power plants being planned [the San Juan Generating Station]. I was working with folks from the Hog Farm and other non-Indians. The urban Navajos said to us, "Why don't you help us organize and educate your people, your society, about Burnham?" Navajo Relocation from Big Mountain was coming up then, too.

So together with the Hog Farm folks, we set up what was called the Burnham–Big Mountain Support Group. There was already one in Albuquerque. One of the main folks there was Mark Rudd, coming out of SDS. Lisa Law was over in Santa Fe, and I was working around here in Oakland and Berkeley with Goose from the Hog Farm and other folks, and we set up a Big Mountain Support Group here. For a number of years the address was my mailbox out in the front yard. It had a big sign on it.

So that was it. I was still doing the urban thing, but instead of working with blacks, I was working with Navajos. I don't think I really understood what I'd been doing with the black community in Detroit until I went down and lived on Indian land, where I finally understood the role of cultural ignorance. I think being down in Indian country, I finally understood what we'd been trying to do in Detroit and why it didn't work. So that meant that I'd better pay attention here and learn from these Navajos.

Our starting point was in the 1980s. The theme for us political lefties was called solidarity. There was real indigenous homegrown revolutionary stuff going on, whether it was Nicaragua, El Salvador, or Big Mountain. Solidarity means that especially for us Anglo folks, it's time to take responsibility for dealing with our government's role in screwing this up. So that's how we understood our Big Mountain work. It was not time for us to go be Indians or El Salvadorans or Nicaraguans. It was time for us to challenge our own government to get right with these people that they're screwing over.

So that was Big Mountain Support.

There were different principles than back in the 1960s and '70s, when there was a lot of confusion as to what's the role of us nonblack, non-Indian folks. During the 1980s, there was a different principle at work that said, "You go deal with your government and get them off our back." It meant that we also understood that it means that it's not for us smart-aleck lefties to bring our analyses here. Our job was to take our direction from the elders, from the indigenous leadership, whether it's in Nicaragua, El Salvador, or Big Mountain. It helped that there were these hard-ass movement folks in AIM who put out a pretty militant message: "You will respect our elders and our people or you're not welcome here."

So that's what we were doing, going down and getting direction from elders. Once a year there was a several-day gathering, and there were shorter visits for organizing material support. We were getting ready for legal support for who's going to be locked up. For the people down there on the land at the time, there were armed confrontations going on and off all the time. Our role wasn't to go join them, but rather to educate our society, our culture, as to what that's about.

It's hard to look back at it because we didn't get done what we wanted to do.

We all knew there was a deadline coming up in 1986 [addressing Navajo Relocation]. We watched the folks on the land organize. They were always in resistance. Starting in '83, '84, '85, '86, the Navajo folks in the Southwest brought the Lakota culture down in the form of a Sun Dance. We were a bunch of semi-lefty Anglos from all over the country, especially the western part of the country. However, we had outposts in Boston and New York. So how do you support ceremonial-based indigenous resistance?

I still don't know how we did. We were invited, some of us, to go be observers. And I think for some of us, going there and being in a support role at a Sun Dance was mind blowing.

By the time we were getting locked up briefly in 1989, after we had our confrontation with the government and it was time for us to go to court, three years past the [1986 Navajo Relocation] deadline, one of the people that came to court with us was Leonard Crow Dog [from South Dakota]. He was one of the leadership elders. He had a real authoritative role. He was part of bringing the Lakota Sun Dance down to Big Mountain.

Leonard came to court with us. There were four of us who had been arraigned, not indicted, but we were up on charges at that point. There was a formal court proceeding where the feds laid out their charges against us as to why we ought to be in jail for violent crimes, fomenting violence.

In the meantime, around the back of the courtroom were people like Roberta Blackgoat and Leonard Crow Dog and a number of the elder women and some of the youth. It was actually kind of daunting. It's like, "Oh my God, they [the Feds] really are seriously going after us."

There was a point during the court proceeding where the prosecutor started babbling. His words were not making sense. And I was sitting there thinking, am I confused or is he confused? By the end of the court proceeding, the judge said, "Well, let me take it under advisement." We didn't know what was going to happen other than we were all coming out of there a little shook up because they seemed serious about locking us up for five years. My daughter was six. At that point I was worried.

So after it was over, we went out and had a big feast. At one point I was standing next to Leonard Crow Dog, and he said, "Did you see what I did to him [the prosecutor]? I just grabbed his spine, and I took it right out."

I had gone down there in 1981 coming from a lefty secular perspective and signed up for an adventure. But I was in for a bigger sleigh ride than that.

Roberta Blackgoat died on April 23, 2002 in San Francisco, where she had continued to battle for the Diné, the Navajo people, till the end of her life. She was eighty-five.

Black Mesa and Big Mountain compose a single landform that lies in the heart of the Colorado Plateau. Between 1970 and 1989, this was the setting where Indian and non-Indian activists collaborated to resist the United States Government's efforts to claim nonrenewable resources from homeland sacred to both Navajo and Hopi cultures. This was yet another expression of Manifest Destiny that had begun well over a century earlier when US military forces waged war relentlessly against American Indians of many cultural persuasions, who were forced to abandon sacred homelands or be exterminated.

The indigenous peoples of the so-called New World have many things to teach the daughters and sons of Europe. To conclude this chapter, I quote what Rina Swentzell (1939–2015) had to say about community and divinity when I interviewed her in 1996.

> We have gotten to the point of too small a definition of community. I go back to the Pueblo thinking, because their community was not just the human community. It included the place within which we lived, so that the mountains were part of community. The water was part of community. Trees, plants, rocks. You know you couldn't have moved through any day in that Old World, even when I was growing up, you couldn't move through it without knowing that you were part of that whole community of trees, rocks, people. Today, what we do is just talk about human community. It gets to be such a small thing, within the larger scope of things. And I think that that is part of the demise of our lives, of modern lives today. We keep making the world smaller and smaller until it is nothing but us. Just human beings. Out of context. Out of our natural context. Out of our cosmological context. We have become so small in our view of the world. Our world is simply us human beings. And that is a crucial point that we need to get beyond, and move back again to seeing ourselves within context.
>
> I think that Pueblo belief in community is all of us together. Because trees are living beings. Rocks are living beings. Water. The spirit moves through the water. An incredible word that we have for the source of life is something that we talk about as the *p'o-wa-ha*. Water-wind-breath. It is there in the water and in the wind that we can see the spirit, that we can see life moving, there where the life force is visible, as well as in the clouds, of course. We don't take the life force and put it in a super human being, as Christians do with God. That already begins to show us the focus on human, and human beings, when you put the life force in a super-human creature—God in superhuman form. But we keep it within the trees, within the water, within the wind, within the clouds. And we are to move through that context, with the water, the wind, and breathe the same breath, to say, "We are breathing the same breath that the rocks do, that the wind does."

And with that, that gives you a totally different feeling. This is it. There is no other reality. We don't go to heaven. We don't leave this dirty world to go to a golden clean heaven. We are here. This is it. This is the world. It doesn't get any better than this. And if we don't honor it in the sense that this is as best, as beautiful, as it is ever going to be, then we can't take care of it if we think that it is a place to be shunned and that we have better things to look forward to. Then we can't walk respectfully where we are at this moment and take care of things and touch things with honor. And breathe each breath. That is what that water-wind-breath is about. Because I mean, my goodness, here it is! And every second I can breathe it in and become a part of this world in no uncertain terms, I am a part of this world that I live in every second, because I believe it every second.

"The Longest Walk," a cross-country walk to draw attention to anti-Indian legislation, 1978. Photo by Seth Roffman.

PART II. FROM THE PAST TO THE FUTURE

15

Counterculture and Environmentalism

JACK LOEFFLER

OVER THE YEARS, I have conducted interviews and recorded music of traditional Indians from as far north as Idaho and as far south as Chiapas, Mexico. Every traditional Indian I've ever met has had deep regard for the sacred quality of homeland. Their respective cultures of practice are aligned with the cycle of the seasons, the flow of nature. These traditional peoples regard themselves as part of the landscape.

In 1996, I visited a traditional Navajo medicine man, or *hataali*, at Navajo Mountain, Utah, in the remotest corner of the Navajo Reservation. This is part of what he said.

> Between the earth, the sun, the moon, it is all related. It is all related to cere-
> monies. It is all in the creation stories. Before humans, before we were made,
> there were only deities, spirits that were here in this world. . . . For us they
> are part of nature that we have to use. We have to get knowledge to take care
> of ourselves, our family, our relatives, and maybe for our society. It is all part
> of it. The sun, the earth, the moon, and everything. . . . After I had my fam-
> ily, I have just become more of a spiritual person. I have more knowledge,
> and the spiritual knowledge that I gain makes me feel very happy and makes
> me feel good and makes me be aware of more of nature. The air, the moun-
> tains, the waters, the plants. This is their prayer. This is their song. And for
> me to have something from nature, that is very powerful to me, that is the
> state of mind to learn for the chanter.

Over a period of four decades I had many conversations with my great friend Alvin Josephy, author and historian of Native America. I recorded Alvin speaking to the Native American perspective in 1984.

> I've talked about the spiritual attachment that the American Indians have
> with the spirits of everything else in creation. Some people call it paganism
> or heathenism; others would call it animism; it's certainly non-Christian.

But that circle of interdependence which maintains harmony and balance is suddenly discovered to be not so dissimilar from the ecological circle in which everything is related. You break one rung of the ecological circle and everything goes awry. Everything in that circle becomes disoriented, loses balance, loses harmony. That, in a way, is the circle of the environmentalists today. They see the interrelationships which they didn't see years ago. They're striving to maintain ecological harmony as well as they can, so it's a new discovery for the White Man, or the European-based person. And yet, it's exactly what the Indian has been doing.

This had already become apparent to me in 1964 when I lived for several months at Navajo Mountain in a traditional Navajo hogan at the invitation of a family of very traditional Navajos. Although we spoke no common language, it was obvious that the Navajo people, the Diné, were profoundly affected by their surrounding homeland. Navajo Mountain rises above the surrounding canyon-carved plateau, the northern edge of which is marked by the San Juan River, the northern boundary of Navajo country. About forty air miles to the south of Navajo Mountain is Black Mesa, an enormous landform whose southern promontories are the First, Second, and Third Mesas, which are home to ancient Hopi Indian villages, some of them inhabited for fifty generations or more. To the Navajos, Black Mesa is the body of the female mountain, and Navajo Mountain is her head. Traditional Hopis believe that they were given permission by Massáu, their powerful deity, to live there and provide spiritual protection to the landscape in all directions. This arid landscape, bounded by the San Juan River to the north, the Río Grande to the east, the Little Colorado River to the south, and the Colorado River to the west, is homeland to both Hopi and Navajo Indians. Subsistence is hard work where rainfall is sparse, where water comes from springs, where gardens are traditionally nurtured in times of drought by carrying water in buckets from the springs.

By 1964, government-drilled wells dotted this landscape, each marked by a windmill, most tapping into the great Pleistocene aquifer that lies beneath Black Mesa. Navajos hauled water in thirty-gallon Army surplus containers from the wells to their hogans either in horse-drawn wagons or occasionally in old pickup trucks. I had one of the very few pickup trucks at Navajo Mountain, and I hauled a lot of water for both my neighbors and myself. A grown man in fair condition can move thirty gallons of contained water from the bed of a pickup truck to the ground.

Although my intimacy with that greater landscape never rivaled that of my Navajo and Hopi friends, I came to know it better than most bilagáanas ("white men" in Navajo) or bahanas ("white men" in Hopi). It was there that I fell deeply in love with our planet, Earth, and began to understand that the sons and daughters of

Europe, who perceived this landscape through secularized vision, were intent on turning as much of it as possible into money. My traditional Indian friends, in contrast, perceived their homeland as sacred, as a living entity of which they were a part.

Five years later, Black Mesa, the Kaibito Plateau, the great Pleistocene aquifer, the Colorado River, the air above the Colorado Plateau, the traditional cultures of the Hopi and Navajo Indians—in short, the heart of the Southwest—were besieged by developers, extractors, government agencies, and giant corporations and their men in government. There was nothing for it but to found the Black Mesa Defense Fund.

Above: *Testimony before the Indian Affairs Subcommittee of the Senate Interior and Insular Affairs against the Black Mesa Mine, Page, Arizona, 1972. Left to right: Thomas Banyacya, Dan Katchungva, Jack Loeffler, David Monongye, and John and Mina Lansa. (Mina was the* kikmongwi, *or leader, of Oraibi.) Photo courtesy of Jack Loeffler.*

Left: *Black Mesa Defense Fund members Jimmy Hopper, Jack Loeffler, and Terrence "Más" Moore, 1971. Photo by Terrence Moore.*

David Brower and Jack Loeffler, Four Corners strip mine, 1972. Photo courtesy of Jack Loeffler.

We were a handful of beatnik-hippies, Hopis, and Navajos, and we didn't understand that we had taken on the Central Arizona Project, regarded by many as a perfect example of collaboration between corporate powers and politicians. The intent was to pump water from the Colorado River over the mountains and into valleys of south-central Arizona, ostensibly for agriculture. Earlier, the CAP had proposed that dams be constructed at either end of the Grand Canyon to generate hydroelectric power to run the pumps. But David Brower and the Sierra Club put a stop to that. The Bureau of Reclamation had already constructed the most contested dam in American history—the Glen Canyon Dam that stoppers the Colorado River downstream from the confluence with the Green and San Juan Rivers to fill Lake Powell—in order to provide a giant reservoir to ensure that the Lower Basin of the Colorado River would receive its apportioned seven and a half million acre feet annually to irrigate the Imperial Valley and provide water to Los Angeles and southern Arizona.

When I conducted an interview with David Brower in the early 1980s, he recalled an even earlier time.

> I knew that it was going to take a great deal of power to move the water up to Central Arizona, a major pumping project. We foresaw way back in the early fifties that this was just a ploy to get water ostensibly for agricultural use but to switch it to domestic use and to industrial use as soon as they could get their hands on it. They were getting it with enormous subsidy. By the time you put the normal interest cost that the government was paying for the money and was not collecting from the farmers who owned a huge subsidy per acre to get the water on it—I did a lot of calculations then— this water was frightfully expensive. We could count on the developers getting hold of the water one way or the other. I did not know the speed with which they were going to do it in Arizona and everywhere else where people started to move because they liked to stay warm.

In 1970, we were working closely with Brower and the Friends of the Earth. Dave was arguably the greatest environmentalist of the twentieth century. He was an avid outdoorsman, and his circle of friends included Allen Ginsberg, Gary Snyder, Jerry Mander, and Michael McClure. One time, Brower and I had been invited into the computer control room at the Four Corners coal-fired power plant in northwestern New Mexico. Brower yelled over at me, "Hey, Loeffler! Did you bring your satchel charge?" We were quickly escorted out of the plant.

It was during this time that Edward Abbey and I began working closely to understand how to stop the sacrifice of the Southwest. In 1968, Ed had published his classic *Desert Solitaire*, wherein he landed hard on the Glen Canyon Dam. We spent many a night camped together on and around Black Mesa scheming how to bring this sacrilege to a halt as he did research for his novel *The Monkey Wrench Gang*, published in 1975.

I recorded Ed Abbey on January 1, 1983—after we had returned from a camping trip in the Superstition Mountains—reflecting on what it might take to turn the juggernaut. Our conversation touched on the definition of terrorism, which is thought provoking more than thirty years later.

> I suppose if political means fail us—public organization and public pressure—if those don't do what has to be done, then we'll be driven to more extreme measures in defending our Earth. Here in the United States, I can see a lot more acts of civil disobedience beginning to occur as the bulldozers and drilling rigs attempt to move into the wilderness and into the back country and the farmlands and the seashores and other precious places. And if civil disobedience is not enough, I imagine there would be sabotage, violence against machinery, property. If that became widespread, it could be that the battle has already been lost. I don't know what would happen beyond that. Such resistance might stimulate some sort of police-state reaction, repression, a real military–industrial dictatorship in this country.
>
> But still, personally, I feel that when all other means fail, we are morally justified—not merely justified, but morally obligated—to defend that which we love by whatever means are available. Just as, if my family, my wife, my children were attacked, I wouldn't hesitate to use violence to defend them. By the same principle, if land I love is being violated, raped, plundered, murdered, and all political means to save it have failed, I personally feel that sabotage is morally justifiable. At least, if it does any good, if it'll help. If it will only help you to feel good.

I would hazard that some would call acts of physical sabotage "terrorism."

> The distinction is quite clear and simple. Sabotage is an act of force or violence against material objects, machinery, in which life is not endangered, or should not be. Terrorism, on the other hand, is violence against living

things—human beings and other living things. That kind of terrorism is generally practiced by governments against their own peoples. Our government committed great acts of terrorism against the people of Vietnam. That's what terrorism means: violence and threats of violence against human beings and other forms of life, which is radically different from sabotage, a much more limited form of conflict. I'd go so far as to say that a bulldozer tearing up a hillside, ripping out trees for a logging operation or a strip mine, is committing terrorism—violence against life.

Dave Foreman, 1984.
Photo by Jack Loeffler.

We lost the battle to thwart the strip mining of coal on Black Mesa. However, as the result of vigorous efforts by southwestern and other environmentalists, the proposed Kaiparowitz coal-fired power plant that would have dwarfed the Four Corners power plant was indeed thwarted. Actor Robert Redford, who was adamantly opposed to the Kaiparowitz plant and strip mine, was burned in effigy. Kaiparowitz was indeed a victory, one of very few, considering the level of environmental activism that had begun to sweep across the land.

In 1980 a new environmental group emerged and soon gained international prominence. Earth First! was founded by Dave Foreman, Howie Wolke, Mike Roselle, and Bart Koehler. Foreman had worked with the Black Mesa Defense Fund and had become a national lobbyist for the Wilderness Society. When I interviewed Dave during the early days of Earth First!, he told me about the book he edited, *Eco Defense: A Field Guide to Monkeywrenching*, with a "Forward!" by Ed Abbey.

It basically comes from the frustration of having worked within the system one way or another as an environmentalist for fifteen years now, as a full-time professional environmentalist, lobbying, working through the agencies, the courts, the whole works, and finding out it's just one big tar baby. The more you try to deal with the system, the more you get stuck in it. Eventually you realize that you aren't going to get anywhere. Yes, you're going to win little victories here and there—you're going to pick up wilderness areas that the system is willing to give you, but the dominant paradigm of our culture and the men running it is to develop every last acre that has anything which they arrogantly call "resources" on it.

I've come to the conclusion that the most effective way to stop this industrial juggernaut is for people individually, acting in true American fashion, to go out and resist it. And you can resist it nonviolently, without danger to yourself or other people, and you can stop it. If you go in and properly pull up survey stakes or help erosion wash out roads that shouldn't be there, sooner or later the Forest Service and other agencies are going to realize that they can't maintain that really expensive infrastructure of roads. A number of things like that will eventually cause the retreat of industrial civilization from millions of acres. I visualize this as simple defense of wilderness.

I sometimes tell people that if you look at the human race not as the consciousness of the Earth, but as the cancer of the Earth, that we're a disease ecologically, and that maybe Nature has evolved some of us as antibodies, that's the only way I can explain why some of us love wilderness and other people have no conception of it at all. And so our role in the future, I think, is to try to preserve as many areas of natural diversity as possible. And hopefully also to develop the ethics and the potential for a human society that can live in harmony with the rest of the planet after this industrial madness burns itself out.

Dave Foreman is also known as an Aldo Leopold scholar and has often referred to the final chapter in Leopold's *Sand County Almanac*, entitled "The Land Ethic." Leopold, who set the stage for the modern environmental movement, advises us to "quit thinking about decent land-use as solely an economic problem. Examine each question in terms of what is ethically and esthetically right, as well as what is economically expedient. A thing is right when it tends to preserve the integrity, stability, and beauty of the biotic community. It is wrong when it tends otherwise."

In 1968, Garrett Hardin published his celebrated essay "The Tragedy of the Commons." He used the example of a commons in Britain where the surrounding inhabitants kept grazing ever more cattle until the herds exceeded the carrying capacity of the commons. Hardin pointed out that the tragedy was that the human population saw in advance that the commons was endangered, but they kept adding cattle anyway.

Four decades later, Elinor Ostrom was awarded the Nobel Prize in economics. Her book *Governing the Commons* introduced the concept of polycentric governance. In an interview, she had this to say.

I use this term of polycentricity, having governing mechanisms at small, medium, large, large-large, however many you have, so that instead of having only the big or only "decentrals," which rarely work, you are developing ways of organizing at multiple levels and then figuring out ways of interrelating so there are some decisions that can be taken at any one of them. There are others that need to be taken at maybe three levels that coordinate.

In other words, governance may take place at various levels, from the grass roots through the county commission through state government all the way to the halls of Congress, rather than just from on high. It requires a high level of mutual cooperation. When dealing with natural resources, or Common Pool Resources at the regional level, grassroots input is vital. To date, centralized governance alone cannot be trusted to have free rein over the fate of the home watershed. Grassroots input is vital for wise governance. My interpretation is that polycentric governance has levels of reciprocity and spreads responsibility more equitably than centralized governance. I also contend that habitat itself must be well represented at every level of human governance. Whether or not we acknowledge this, the bottom line is that the ecosystem itself has the last word by either being able to sustain the carrying capacity or crashing.

Poet and philosopher Gary Snyder has inspired three generations of readers. Here are his thoughts from a 1985 conversation about bioregionalism, a concept that had begun to gain currency among countercultural environmentalists more than a decade earlier.

> "Bioregion," the term itself, would refer to a region that is defined by its plant and animal characteristics, its life-zone characteristics that flow from soil and climate: the territory of Douglas fir or the region of coastal redwoods, short-grass prairie, medium-grass prairie, and tall-grass prairie; high desert and low desert. Those could be bioregional definitions. When you get more specific, you might say Northern Plains short-grass prairie, upper Missouri watershed, or some specific watershed of the upper Missouri. The criteria are flexible, but even though the boundaries and delineations can vary according to your criteria, there is roughly something we all agree upon. Just like we agree on what a given language is, even though languages are fluid in their dialects. So bioregionalism is kind of a creative branch of the environmental movement that strives to re-achieve indigeneity, re-achieve aboriginality, by learning about the place and what really goes on there.
>
> Bioregionalism goes beyond simple geography or biology by its cultural concern, its human concern. It is to know not only the plants and animals of a place, but also the cultural information of how people live there—the ones who know how to do it. Knowing the deeper mythic, spiritual, archetypal implications of a fir, or a coyote, or a blue jay might be to know from both inside and outside what the total implications of a place are. So it becomes not only a study of place, but a study of psyche in place. That's what makes it so interesting. In a way, it seems to me that it's the first truly concrete step

that has been taken since Kropotkin in stating how we decentralize ourselves after the twentieth century.

Decentralization, as Ostrom and Snyder understand, is one of the most important issues of our time. We are currently governed almost exclusively from the top down. Much of our legislation serves corporate interests in its quest for access to natural resources to increase fiscal wealth by pursuing quantitative growth. The counterculture spawned the modern environmental movement to inhibit growth for its own sake, as well as to protect natural habitat for the sake of nurturing biodiversity, preserving wilderness. Today, the government of the United States is failing to react to the enormity of the environmental crises that we have spawned on our planet. This failing is not restricted to our governing body. It is a cultural failing as well. We have forgotten the lessons of indigenous Americans and the counterculture. We have separated ourselves from our understanding of our place in Nature.

Polycentric governance as Ostrom defines it can reinvigorate cooperation both within our species and with the land. Bioregionalism and watershed thinking also suggest means of cultural recovery within the context of habitat. Governance from on high has resulted in faulty legislation. Grassroots governance is a sane alternative. This means that there must be a large measure of decentralized governance, governance that grows from within the watershed, the bioregion. In my opinion, the watershed, the bioregion, should metaphorically sit at the head of the table of any governing body. All species should be well represented at that table. In this way, the human species may come to recognize that reciprocity and mutual cooperation are vital to continuity and ecosystemic health.

Fritjof Capra, originally trained as a quantum physicist, is widely known for his 1975 book *The Tao of Physics*. This book had great appeal for many counterculturalists who were delighted to perceive an intelligent relationship between ancient Chinese philosophy and modern science. Capra gradually undertook the study of ecology and biology and in 2014 published, with collaborator Pier Luisi Luigi, *The Systems View of Life: A Unifying Vision*. A superb study in how ecology works, this book provides a compelling and comprehensive presentation of the interrelationships and interconnectedness between all life forms. In 2014, I spent a day with Fritjof Capra and recorded this statement.

The last part of our book *The Systems View of Life* is about the practical implications of the systems view, and it is called *Sustaining the Web of Life*. It has three chapters. One is a chapter on ecology, the history and the basic principles of ecology and sustainability. The second chapter is a systemic assessment of the problems of our time, which are all interconnected and therefore are systemic problems. At the very root, in my view of these systemic problems, is our obsession with unlimited growth, unlimited quantitative economic growth, which is of course an illusion because on a finite planet, not everything can grow.

And so this illusion of perpetual growth is something that I want to counteract with the concept of qualitative growth. The basic idea is that when you see that economic growth really is the motor of capitalism, the motor of overconsumption and therefore of waste, of pollution, of species extinction, the maldistribution of wealth, the economic inequality—all this is driven by this obsession with economic and corporate growth.

In Europe especially, there's a movement of no growth, of negative growth. I believe that this cannot be held up because when you look at life, you see that growth is a fundamental property of life. All living systems grow. But not everything grows at the same time. So in an ecosystem, certain parts will decline and disintegrate. Their elements will then be liberated and be used as resources for further growth.

So qualitative growth would be a system where certain parts in the economy would be allowed to grow but other parts would have to decline. So we need to distinguish between good growth and bad growth. Of course, from an ecological point of view, that distinction is very simple. Growth that increases global warming, growth that uses nonrenewable resources, that uses toxics, that pollutes the air, that destroys community, that increases economic inequality, is bad growth, and the growth that does the opposite is good growth. So that's how we need to qualify growth. I've been fascinated by the fact that this idea of qualitative growth is very consistent with the systems view of life, which is a science of qualities. So there is a shift from quantity to quality, both in science and in this notion of growth.

Melissa Savage, 2016.
Photo by Jack Loeffler.

Melissa Savage is a biogeographer who earned her PhD at the University of Colorado in Boulder. She was a faculty member at UCLA until she retired and founded the Four Corners Institute in New Mexico. For many years, she has been restoring river otters to their appropriate habitats. Here, she describes how she became involved with the modern environmental movement, not long after she first arrived in San Francisco in 1967.

Actually I think I got there [San Francisco] in the late spring and that was the Summer of Love. Things had been percolating along for a long time. They started in the late 1950s really in a very small way. I was, like so many of my generation, completely ready to be open to what was going on. There were so many of us. There were so many people doing so many kinds of things. The way I experienced San Francisco counterculture at that time was that it included many braided strands of involvement, and I immediately got involved in the environmental aspect of it. But across the bay there were the Black Panthers in full swing and there were SDS [Students for a Democratic Society] people. Many of these strands had very little overlap with one another, but what they all had in common was against-the-mainstream culture.

That's one of the reasons why the term "counterculture" has relevance for me, also "subculture." The subculture always exists. And I really think of the roots of the Sixties subculture as starting nearly a century before with the bohemians. This theme in human culture has been around for a long time, in Western culture anyway. So I got involved with Keith Lampe, who had changed his name to Ponderosa Pine, which was an outrageous thing to do. And he was sending out a newsletter once a month that was pretty radical environmental thinking to a group of his addressees that he thought would hear the message. They weren't soliciting his message.

So I was plunged immediately into the more radical part of the environmental movement. And he was very good friends with Gary Snyder, and Gary would come to the house and sit and talk with other people about the philosophy of the movement. And I remember sitting in the shadows and listening to conversations among maybe five people, including Gary, in which they were developing the basis for the little document called *The Four Changes* that captured for me—and that was probably in 1969—where radical environmentalism was at, at that moment.

And then of course as you know, we got involved in other publications. I was an editor at *Clear Creek* [magazine] in probably 1970. We were soliciting articles from everybody who was relevant to the topic, including poets. Gary and the northern California poets were a tremendous impetus to the environmental movement.

The environmental stream in the counterculture movement that was going on then in San Francisco was different from hippies. Hippies were their own stream. These were the kind of Back to the Land people who moved out into the country. Peter Coyote was one of these people, and I remember he was planning for the revolution. There was a kind of a cultural revolution around Back to the Land, being able to get in touch with what sustained you in life: food, water. And that stream, like all the streams of the counterculture, continued right through the seventies, the eighties, the nineties, till right now. Wendell Berry is a wonderful spokesman for what used to be the original thought behind the hippie movement, the Back to the Land movement. But that was a different kind of thing from the environmental movement, which was very activist and intended to make big changes through cultural revolution in the way people related to the environment. That energy spread out over the cultural landscape in the decades afterwards.

I believe that Nature needs indigenous mind to continue during this time of human domination of habitat. I've worked from that premise my whole life long. Does that recognition of the presence of traditional indigenous people's perspective ring a bell with you?

We have had the benefit of being able to experience indigenous mind here [in New Mexico]. Pueblo people in particular are so articulate about their view. "We are going to be here in a thousand years, in two thousand years, and that's how we relate to our environment and to our land and our landscapes." We sure don't have that perspective in the Anglo [culture] now, because we're always moving around, we have very little loyalty to our landscapes. And that was one of the great themes with the counterculture, you know: connect to the land wherever you are. Connect to the place where you are. And that has borne fruit in the bioregional movement. But the Indians have been here for a very long time. They've always been connected to their place. So that was important to me.

And even more important for me is understanding the indigenous point of view about, for lack of a better word, sentient beings. For them everything around them is sentient, is people. The world is full of people: lizard people and aspen people and mockingbird people. It's not just human people. It's all those other people. And I think that has carried over from American Indian culture in a kind of emerging strand in the environmental movement and even the mainstream movement, and that is a new appreciation and respect for other forms of life, which has mattered a lot to me. I work on the conservation of otters, and my experience of otters is that they are people like us, and I see them behave in all those ways that people behave: they're playful and they're fierce and they love one another and they kick each other around. They have an experience on earth that is like my experience on earth. And I think that has definitely filtered through the Native American Indian culture into ours. And I think that during the twenty-first century, there's going to be a sea change in the way we see the other people of the world besides human people.

Over the last half-century, the ancient concept of the commons has reemerged in our consideration of the land. The late Rina Swentzell from the Tewa Pueblo of Santa Clara spoke to me of her understanding of the commons.

From a Pueblo point of view, the commons is everything. It is the context that we live in. Again, when I talk about it, it's the old Pueblo thinking. The community was always thought of as being whole. Everything was interconnected. There was always a center to it as well, and I was a center and you were a center. There were many centers as a part of the whole thing. And we think that a whole has one center. In a way it's true. But with the Pueblo there are so many simultaneous things that can happen at once, which is all part of the commons, I think, because there are so many things that go on at the same time. The wind is blowing, the water's flowing, and we're actually walking around and talking. It's all part of this idea of what we all share. It's that notion of sharing.

In that Pueblo context, then, the focus was always, What is it that surrounds me? Who and what surrounds me, and who do I work with and around all the time? The primary thing is that it was the earth, the sky, the clouds, the wind, and that incredible term that we have that for me says it all: it's the p'o-wa-ha, it's the water-wind-breath. The thing that we're feeling right now. And that connects, it moves through our entire world in such a way that it connects everybody and everything. That becomes the commons in a sense. It's that real ethereal thing. What is that blowing through the window right now that's giving us all vitality actually? That's the flow of life. In the Pueblo it really was that thing that swirls around, that swirls, that moves, that creates that sense of commons. It's the ultimate of what is common to every living being. What do we have in common with the trees, with the rocks, with all of that that makes our life what it is today?

The p'o-wa-ha is something that moves through us all. It not only flows through me, it flows through you, it flows through the plants outside. It moves the clouds around. It moves the waters. It's there. That's the kinship. We are all participating in this flowing water-wind in the breath. And it's the breath that becomes the commons then. It is the breath. It's that flowing air that becomes the commons. When you talk about kinship, the ant doesn't breathe it any better than I do. It doesn't like the ant any better than it likes me. I am flowing with it and so is the ant. To the degree that I acknowledge that I am breathing in that p'o-wa-ha, I become a more aware person because I can see that my kinship to the ant is very, very essential, is very real. It's the real thing. It's what connects us all.

Gary Paul Nabhan. Photo by Jack Loeffler.

16

The Bohemian-Hip-n-Beat
Beginnings of Counter (Agri-)Culture

BROTHER COYOTE, OEF (GARY PAUL NABHAN)

I'm goin' up the country, baby don't you wanna go?
　　—Canned Heat, "Going up the Country"

TEXAS BLUESMAN HENRY THOMAS recorded "Bull Doze Blues" in 1928, but it took another forty years for Canned Heat to turn it into "Going up the Country," the rural hippie anthem that gave the Back to the Land movement its battle cry.

By the time Canned Heat gave back-to-the-landers their song, less than half the world's population lived beyond the urban fringe, and less than 2 percent of the North American public lived in rural areas outside towns, cities, and suburbs. But a new agrarianism was suddenly being ushered in, not restricted to the rural domain and not simply a romantic desire to reenact social behaviors and mores associated with rural populaces in bygone eras.

Instead, the new agrarianism emerging from American countercultures hit pay dirt within urban, as well as rural, communities. It seemed to foster a set of values and operating principles that could obliterate the rural-urban divide that, in many ways, had characterized and crippled North American and European cultures during much of the twentieth century.

But what exactly does "agrarian counterculture" mean? In the ancient kindred term "agri-culture," based on the Latin *ager + colere*, we see the relationship between humans and the land circumscribed by the *radical* (read: deeply rooted) activities and values of cultivating, tilling, stewarding, tending, and safeguarding.

Since the countercultural convergence, agrarianism has come to embody a nuanced set of social, political, and ecological values that see rural activities, behaviors, and ethics as functioning on a higher order than urban- or suburban-derived comparables. However, for well over a century, the phrase "agrarian reform" has had broader recognition in Latin America, Europe, and Asia as a movement to keep peasant societies from becoming increasingly landless and in greater servitude to capitalistic institutions by enacting the redistribution of land and other wealth. The American school of new agrarianism, like these other schools with which it converged, was a *movement of resistance*.

Many bohemians, beatniks, and hippies had raged against the machine in the sixties and early seventies, without much luck in placing their monkey wrenches into the cogs of the Killing Wheel at the right place and the right time. And so they headed for green pastures, carrying with them a *Whole Earth Catalog*, Rodale's *Encyclopedia of Organic Gardening*, and maybe, for the younger ones, copies of Wendell Berry's *Farming: A Handbook* or *The Unsettling of America*.

One long-haired doomsday journalist I knew in spring of 1970 at the first Earth Day Headquarters was sure that civilization as we knew it would collapse within a year's time. So he bought a backpack, a sleeping bag, some work boots, and a pair of OshKosh B'gosh overalls, threw all the paper in his office into a recycling bin, walked down the middle of Constitution Avenue and then out to Dulles Airport. He bought a ticket to Alaska with his last bit of cash and immediately flew to Anchorage, where he hitchhiked back into hinterlands between there and Fairbanks. (We know those landscapes today as the place where Sarah Palin hallucinated Russia from her doorstep.)

Dr. Longhair told me he was going "back to the land" to homestead until the military-political-industrial complex vanished from the face of the earth. Of course, by the time he got up to Alaska, the place was already crawling with oil prospectors, surveyors, and construction engineers heading to Prudhoe Bay, hoping to build the great Alaska pipeline. Nevertheless, Longhair still had a few weeks after Earth Day until the frost-free season to study up on how to grow food and plant a few seeds of "herb" in Dixie cups full of soil on his windowsill.

In his spare time, he read issues of *Organic Gardening* and *Mother Earth News* in community health clinic waiting rooms. He found copies of Helen and Scott Nearing's books in the public library and fell asleep reading them. Thumbing through Euell Gibbons's books on stalking wild foods made him hungry for home, thirsty for spring.

He declared himself a homesteader before he planted a single vegetable seed or sapling, but he was ornery enough to persist and smart enough to try to learn what he didn't know. Fortunately, it got better from there.

There were thousands if not tens of thousands much like him, fleeing the cities, then going up the country to cultivate home-grown tomatoes and railroad weed. Some went off to apprentice with the madman of Green Gulch and Santa Cruz, Alan Chadwick. Others tracked down Mildred Loomis at Lane's End Farm in Ohio or later at the Heathcote Center in Maryland.

Those in the Southwest flocked to see Peter van Dresser, who moved to a small village in the mountains of northern New Mexico in 1949 to open a little "local" restaurant, design solar- and wind-powered houses, and work on landscape-level agrarian development of decentralized, self-sufficient communities.

Still others hung with Dr. Ralph Borsodi in Suffern, New York, who tried to teach people how to live the "good life" in trying times, while tossing out ideas like "alternative currencies" as if they were dollar bills counterfeited by Coyote the Trickster.

All these ingredients got thrown into one big pot of slumgullion stew that changed flavor and texture over time. The Back to the Land movement turned into the organic gardening and regenerative agriculture initiative, which morphed into new alchemy aquaponics and sustainable agriculture, which then mutated into the permaculture movement, the one-straw revolution, the perennial polyculture, the farming-the-wild initiative, and the paradigm shift into slow food, slow money, slow water, and slow church.

These hubs of the new agrarian movement had their high priests and visionaries, some of whom truly earned their notoriety: Robert Rodale and Gene Logsdon, Wendell Berry and Wes Jackson, John Todd, Nancy Todd and William McLarney, Alan Chadwick and John Jeavons, Douglas Stevenson and Steve Gaskin, Abbie Page McMillan and Eliot Coleman, and Alan Kapuler and Forest Roth-Shomer, as well as welcomed foreigners such as Masanobou Fukuoka and Bill Mollison.

Wendell Berry's *Mad Farmer* poems and yarns were not written with hyperbole in mind. They exuded the crazy agrarian contrarianism of that era. Keep in mind that Berry himself did time outside Kentucky, paying his dues in Wallace Stegner's creative writing workshop at Stanford during the same general era that Ken Kesey, Ed Abbey, Gurney Norman, Ed McClanahan, Raymond Carver, Tom McGuane, Larry McMurtry, and Hunter S. Thompson were mulling and sniffing around the same campus. Organic vegetables were not the only items that these boys ingested during that formative era.

Soon, agrarian networks spread like underground mycelia in various bioregions. In the Northeast, the Maine Organic Farmers and Gardeners Association became the first such continuous presence. Tilth in the Northwest soon followed. EcoFarm in California, NOFA in New England, MOSES in the Midwest, PASA in Pennsylvania, the Quivira Coalition in the Southwest, and the Ogallala Commons in the southern Great Plains emerged in one form or another as time went on.

The role these ad hoc grassroots agrarian networks had in moving the cultural communities of their regions toward some sort of place-based sustainability cannot be overstated. New leaders in community economics emerged out of them: David Orr, Francis Moore Lappé, Elizabeth Henderson, Paul Hawken, Marty Strange, Stephanie Mills, George Ballis, Maurice Telleen, David Kline, Susan Witt, Judy Wicks, Woody Tasch, Johnny Sundstrom, William Kittredge, Stanley Crawford, Joel Salatin, Fred Kirschenmann, David Masamoto, Juan Estevan Arrellano, Albert Bates, Ari Weinzweig, and Sandor Katz, to name a few.

What has become obvious is that many of the innovations first promulgated by this band of agrarian creatives were initially ignored, dismissed, or derided by academia, government, and, most especially, mainstream agriculture. But within less than two decades, many agroecological practices once considered to be "outlandish" have been documented, tested, tried, refined, and then validated in USDA field stations, land grant universities, and private experimental farms around the country and around the world.

Today, whole departments and institutes have cropped up in academia to train farmers in how to incorporate seed diversity, agroecology, and low-input "organic" practices into commercial farming on a scale unimaginable in the 1970s. But this should not surprise us: innovations typically come in from the scrappy margins of society rather than from the well-funded institutions in the mainstream, where bureaucrats are usually too busy raising funds in order to meet the expectations of the status quo practitioners rather than taking substantial risks to meet the expectations of the land.

A half-century later, the Young Agrarians, the Greenhorns, the Farm Hackers, the Farm Folk/City Folk, and the Guerilla Grafters are taking the whole agrarian road show to places it couldn't or wouldn't go when old beatniks, hippies, peaceniks, trustafarians, and ancient agrarians were driving the bus of Merry Pranksters.

That circling back and renewal is important since Americans seem to suffer from (Agri-)Cultural Alzheimer's: they seem to forget that what they are doing today had any precedents before Al Gore invented the Internet.

Whenever we forget that we've sandblasted away most of the traditional farming communities on this planet that survived into the late twentieth century, someone remembers that we can still listen to the plants and animals themselves regardless of how many of the Old Ways have survived. We're like the Ol' Sassy Dolls in *Mad Max: Fury Road*, who have become the Keepers of the Seeds and are willing to kick Any Man's ass if he tries to steal them, patent them, or tweak them into GMOs.

If the Old Seeds won't always work in the Coming [read: Present] Era of Global Weirding, we can all jump on board the algae-fueled wagon of Biomimicry and try to redesign all our food systems "as if nature really mattered." Or as if our ten-thousand-year-old agrarian traditions carried with them an indefatigable spirit.

As the parents of the assassinated indigenous protesters in Iguala, Michoacán, recently proclaimed on their placards, "They tried to bury us, but they forgot that we are seeds."

The agrarian revolution is still in metamorphosis and is not only reinhabiting wounded rural lands but will soon be showing up at an inner city theater near you, thanks to Sim VanderRyn, Karen Washington, John Jeavons, Alice Waters, Will

Allen, Cashawn Myers and Severine von Tscharner Fleming, and a host of other died-in-the-wool Locavores of all colors and classes.

Today the demography of farming is far different from what it was in the 1970s. One in every five American farmers is a woman; Asian, Hispanic, and Native American farmers are increasing in number, while many Anglo and African Americans have already left the land. Eighty percent of the food harvested in fields, orchards, truck gardens, feedlots, and greenhouses in the United States is brought to you from soil to table by Mexican Americans, many of whom are undocumented, under age, uninsured, and virtually homeless. Climate change and political refugees emigrating from Somalia, Ethiopia, the Sudan, and Syria are adding their own flavors to the American agrarian movement.

Nevertheless, all of those cultures who bring Americans their daily bread are among the likeliest to need to go through bread lines, food pantries, and soup kitchens to feed their own families. If there is one food issue that the counterculture movement has not been able to solve on its own, it is that of providing other American cultures broader safety nets and chances to break through the glass ceiling to become farmers on their own.

We will know such a goal has been achieved when no one takes the current tagline of the American Farm Bureau Federation—the NRA of conventional agriculture—seriously any more. It purports to be "*the* Voice of American Agriculture" in a world where thousands of diverse voices are needed as part of a resonant choir.

Brown Berets in Santa Fe. Photo courtesy of the Center for Southwest Research, University Libraries, University of New Mexico.

University of New Mexico protest escalates in response to Kent State shootings, 1970. Photo courtesy of the Center for Southwest Research, University Libraries, University of New Mexico.

17

Ebb Tide

JACK LOEFFLER

THROUGH THE AGES, countercultures have been marked by a refusal of governance from on high, a hatred of bureaucracy, a profound strain of anarchism, a thread of paganism. I've come to understand that counterculturalists have often taken their cues from the flow of Nature. I certainly have, and I try to meditate on that on a daily basis as I sit beside the trail breathing the clear air of high country New Mexico, recognizing my kindred-ness with all the species around me. This is the basis of my own sense of spirituality and fundamental to my practice of counterculture.

What influenced the late-twentieth-century wave of counterculture? For many, counterculture was a reaction to the spiritual malaise and rise of consumerism and imperialism that permeated post–World War II America. For others, it was a reaction to the extreme heedlessness of civil rights by our nation both here and abroad. US military forces terrorized the people of Vietnam. Blacks, Hispanos, and American Indians experienced abuse at the hands of the general citizenry, political extremists, and government under corporate control. Thus, the antiwar movement, the Black Panther Party, the Chicano movement, and the American Indian Movement gained vigorous momentum.

The modern environmental movement was born out of the counterculture in recognition of our greatest jeopardy: we have trashed our planet to the edge of oblivion for many species, including us, Homo sapiens. Revolutionaries of every ilk have adapted themselves to combat the forces of the corporate-military-political-industrial complex. Scientists, beatniks, hippies, outdoors men and women, adventurers, artists, writers, musicians, farmers, ranchers, veterans, mechanics, grocery clerks, and museum curators have become passionate environmentalists. A fair number, as this book shows, have tried to emulate American Indians, many of whom are still deeply integrated within indigenous mind and cannot fathom the plunder of sacred landscape for the sake of turning habitat into money.

Just what is indigenous mind? Indigenous mind is cultural consciousness shaped by the flow of nature through home habitat, the recognition of the biotic community, the sense of kinship with all other life forms, recognition of the sacred in all of creation. It has evolved over our two hundred thousand years of species-hood but is gradually being subsumed by the rise and spread of civilization over the last nine thousand years or so. Indigenous mind continues to exist within land-based traditional cultures, including American Indians.

The longing to return to the indigenous mindset inspired much of the counterculture movement. A major thrust of counterculturists has been immersion in the flow of nature, thereby honoring traditional indigenous cultures that have survived in spite of centuries of contempt, neglect, and suppression. Edward Abbey's take on our relationship to nature is eloquent.

> I regard the invention of monotheism and the other-worldly God as a great setback for human life. . . . Once we took the gods out of Nature, out of the hills and forests around us, and made all those little gods into one great god up in the sky, somewhere in outer space, why about then human beings, particularly Europeans, began to focus our attention on transcendental values, a transcendental deity, which led to a corresponding contempt for Nature and the world which feeds and supports us. From that point of view, I think the Indians and most traditional cultures had a much wiser world view, in that they invested every aspect of the world around them—all of Nature—animal life, plant life, the landscape itself, with gods, with deity. In other words, everything was divine in some way or another. Pantheism probably led to a much wiser way of life, more capable of surviving over long periods of time.

One of the finer countercultural moments in defense of Indian culture that I have been witness to and participated in was one afternoon in 1980 when former Arizona congressman and secretary of the interior Stewart Udall shared the stage in the Paolo Soleri outdoor amphitheater in Santa Fe with folk musician Pete Seeger, author Edward Abbey, and musicians Eliza Gilkyson and the Family Lotus. The master of ceremonies was John Kimmey. Pete Seeger sang his heart out, mesmerizing the audience, dancing to the beat of his own music. Ed Abbey read from his novel *The Monkey Wrench Gang* and inspired 1,200 members of the audience to "resist much, obey little." The purpose of the concert was to raise funds for Stewart Udall to compensate Navajo Indian uranium miners and their widows. Stewart spoke about the Navajo miners, who were not informed of the consequences of descending deep beneath the surface of the Earth to dig out uranium to be used for construction of nuclear weapons and as fuel for nuclear energy. Miners died, and many others fell prey to radiation sickness. Stewart devoted much of the rest of his life to fighting for the families of these uranium miners by engaging in legal combat with the government that he had served first as a belly gunner in the US Army Air Corps, then as a congressman from Arizona, and finally as the greatest secretary of the interior that our nation has yet known.

Top left: *Stewart Udall at the Paolo Soleri Amphitheater as part of the Stewart Udall fundraiser for Navajo Indian uranium miners and widows, Santa Fe, 1980. Photo by Seth Roffman.* Top right: *Edward Abbey reading from the* Monkey Wrench Gang, *Paolo Soleri Amphitheater, Stewart Udall fundraiser for Navajo Indian uranium miners and widows, Santa Fe, 1980. Photo by Seth Roffman.* Bottom: *Eliza Gilkyson, Paolo Soleri Amphitheater, Stewart Udall fundraiser for Navajo Indian uranium miners and widows, Santa Fe, 1980. Photo by Seth Roffman.*

David Monongye and Eliza Gilkyson, Santa Fe, 1970s. Photo by Seth Roffman.

Pete Seeger with the Family Lotus and Jack Loeffler (on trumpet) performing at the Paolo Soleri Amphitheater, Stewart Udall fundraiser for Navajo Indian uranium miners and widows, Santa Fe, 1980. Photo by Seth Roffman.

My friend Reno Kleen Myerson and I were privileged to produce that concert. Although all of us who were involved in that 1980 concert in Santa Fe came with diverse cultural and political perspectives, each of us was inspired by that countercultural, environmental, and political zeal born of mutual recognition that we have to react relentlessly against the deadly juggernaut that continues to prevail to this day.

Moments such as these should occur with far greater regularity in this cultural time zone. If we're going to Be Here Now, we must now be here as consciously as we can.

Hearkening back to the 1950s, '60s, '70s, and '80s, I realize how much American Indians, especially in the Southwest, influenced the counterculture movement. They welcomed us into their peyote ceremonies and opened our hearts and minds to new levels of perception and clarity, especially regarding the sacred quality of the landscape. They opened our eyes to how monoculture has secularized habitat. They made us aware that our monocultural attitudes and practices are at loggerheads with Nature's way. They showed that Nature is its own reason to be. The extent to which American Indians have remained in touch with their traditions in the face of monoculture sets an example for countercultures.

The counterculture has now been absorbed into the greater cultural fabric. But the environmental juggernaut looms ever larger. Only the ignorant ignore climatic instability, human overpopulation, waning natural resources like water (water? yes, water) and thus arable land on which to produce food, the growing likelihood of pandemic, the extinction of species, the endless wars based on conflicting ideologies and maneuvers to claim what's left of nonrenewable resources. And just who are these ignorant human beings who so ignore the reality of the present? We all are.

Many political leaders worldwide have finally realized that too much carbon dioxide in the atmosphere can destroy the planetary habitat as we know it. Great nations such as China and the United States are finally taking gigantic steps to reduce pollution in the atmosphere. Scientists are working to streamline a new technological era and to correct earlier technologies.

But science alone will not save us from ourselves. Again, my friend Ed Abbey had something important to say about the future.

> I think by virtue of reason, common sense, the evidence of our five good bodily senses, and daily experience, we can imagine a better way to live, with fairly simple solutions. Not easy—but simple. Beginning here in America—we should set the example. We have set the example for pillaging the planet and we should set the example for preserving life, including human life. First, most important, reduce human numbers, gradually, by normal attrition. Reduce the human population to a reasonable number, a self-sustaining number. . . . And then, second, simplify our needs and demands, so that we're not preying to excess on other forms of life—plant life and animal life—by developing new attitudes, a natural reverence for all forms of life.

Ed's words reflect wisdom inherent in indigenous mind, the knowledge of countless generations of American Indians who have inhabited this continent for thousands of years. Our greatest challenge is to identify and adopt a new system of attitudes in harmony with the flow of Nature. Our species has thrown life for all species out of balance. What does common sense, the evidence of our five good bodily senses, our intellect, our intuition, reveal to us? What system of attitudes need we adopt to Be Here Now in such a way as to allow our children, their children, and future generations to Be Here Then? We can apply awareness from throughout the ages that meets our current challenges. It is imperative that we shift from an economically dominated cultural paradigm to an ecologically motivated system of attitudes.

In the meantime, hiking a trail through countryside or a city park is a first step into a new attitude about where we live. Acknowledging plants and fellow creatures along the trail invigorates a sense of kindred. Reflecting on Nature's complexity is, at least for me, a joyful and profound experience. To jump into a hot spring naked, to eat food from your own garden, to get high in spite of the law, to make love under the stars, to play music, to create a painting, to write a verse, to meditate on emptiness, to live within your own evolving system of ethics—all contribute to balance within the flow of Nature.

The great recent wave of counterculture is now at its ebb. A new counterculture could come from the young, a generation that tweets, blogs, and perfects social networking. But I would hope that the natural world would not be excluded, that bioregionalism and watershed thinking would become much of the basis for a new system of attitudes. Can we come to understand that habitat itself must be clearly represented at the head of the table of any governing body? I would also hope that governance would become more polycentric, including governance from the grass roots rather than purely centralized governance from on high. Can we recognize that the Divine Right of Kings has largely become the corporate right of first refusal?

Much of past countercultural perspective has been focused on humans and inequities born of human social injustice. The modern environmental movement has expanded this focus to ecological thinking The stage is set for the next wave of counterculture. It is eagerly anticipated. At its heart lies reverence for life and consciousness. The next wave will be inspired by the inheritors of the present, hopefully with enthusiasm. Enthusiasm is the energy that powers imagination, and imagination is vital to the pursuit of counterculture. Always remember that the practice of counterculture itself is an art form, a manifestation from within the commons of consciousness, nurtured by the flow of Nature.

In consciousness we trust!

Folk musician Jim Bowie of the Family Lotus at the Santa Fe Plaza, 1970s. Photo by Seth Roffman.

FURTHER READING

Abbey, Edward	*Desert Solitaire* *The Monkey Wrench Gang*
Berry, Wendell	*The Unsettling of America*
Brand, Stewart	*Whole Earth Catalog, 1968–1972*
Brandi, John	*The World, the World* *Reflections in a Lizard's Eye: Notes from the High Desert* *Into the Dream Maze*
Campbell, Joseph	*The Hero with a Thousand Faces*
Capra, Fritjof	*The Tao of Physics: An Exploration of the Parallels between Modern Physics and Eastern Mysticism*
Capra, Fritjof, and Pier Luigi Luisi	*The Systems View of Life: A Unifying Vision*
Castaneda, Carlos	*The Teachings of Don Juan: A Yaqui Way of Knowledge*
Chuang Tzu	*The Complete Works of Chuang Tzu*
Coyote, Peter	*Sleeping Where I Fall: A Chronicle* *The Rainman's Third Cure: An Irregular Education*
Crawford, Stanley	*Mayordomo*
de Angulo, Jaime	*Indian Tales*
deBuys, William	*A Great Aridness* *Seeing Things Whole: The Essential John Wesley Powell* *River of Traps*
Deloria, Vine	*Custer Died for Your Sins: An Indian Manifesto*

Foreman, Dave	*Take Back Conservation*
	Confessions of an Eco-warrior
	The Big Outside
Ginsberg, Allen	*Howl and Other Poems*
Goffman, Ken, and Dan Joy	*Counterculture through the Ages: From Abraham to Acid House*
Hardin, Garrett	*The Tragedy of the Commons*
	An Ecolate View of the Human Predicament
Harner, Michael	*The Way of the Shaman*
Hesse, Herman	*Siddhartha*
	Steppenwolf
	Magister Ludi
Huxley, Aldous	*The Doors of Perception*
	Island
unattributed	*The I Ching, or Book of Changes*
Jackson, Wes	*Consulting the Genius of Place*
Jeffers, Robinson	*The Beginning and the End*
Josephy, Alvin M.	*Red Power: The American Indians' Fight for Freedom*
	Now That the Buffalo's Gone
Julyan, Robert	*The Place Names of New Mexico*
Kahn, Lloyd	*Shelter*
Keltz, Iris	*Scrapbook of a Taos Hippie*
Kerouac, Jack	*On the Road*
	The Dharma Bums
Klein, Ben	*Irwin Klein and the New Settlers*
Kopecky, Art	*New Buffalo: Journals from a Taos Commune*
	Leaving New Buffalo Commune
Kroeber, A. L.	*Cultural and Natural Areas of Native North America*
Kropotkin, Peter	*Mutual Aid*
	Kropotkin's Revolutionary Pamphlets

Roszak, Theodore	*The Making of a Counter Culture*
Rudnick, Lois	*Utopian Vistas: The Mabel Dodge Luhan House and the American Counterculture*
Sakaki, Nanao	*How to Live on the Planet Earth* *Real Play*
Shepard, Paul	*Coming Home to the Pleistocene*
Smith, Sherry	*Hippies, Indians, and the Fight for Red Power*
Snyder, Gary	*Turtle Island* *Riprap and Cold Mountain Poems* *The Practice of the Wild* *The Gary Snyder Reader*
Steen, Athena Swentzell, and Bill Steen	*The Straw Bale House*
Suzuki, D. T.	*Essays in Zen Buddhism*
Thoreau, Henry David	*Resistance to Civil Government*
Tolkien, J. R. R.	*The Lord of the Rings* (Trilogy)
Twain, Mark	*The Adventures of Huckleberry Finn*
Watts, Alan	*The Way of Zen*
Whalen, Philip	*On Bear's Head* *Heavy Breathing*
Whitman, Walt	"This is what you shall do," from the 1855 preface to *Leaves of Grass*
Wilkinson, Charles	*Fire on the Plateau*
Williams, Terry Tempest	*Refuge: An Unnatural History of Family and Place*
Wilson, Edward O.	*Biophilia* *The Diversity of Life*
Woodcock, George	*Anarchism: A History of Libertarian Ideas and Movements*

INDEX

Page numbers in *italics* refer to illustrations.

Trudell, John, 158, *159*, 160

Udall, Stewart, 192, *193*
United Indians of All Tribes, 158
University of California, Berkeley, 43–44
US Forest Service, 15, 17, 20, 31–32, 177
US government, 30, 53, 81, 101, 174, 188; and environmental crises, 178–79; and Native Americans, 25–26, 76, 162, 164–66, 172–73, 192; opposition to, 42–43, 76, 79, 162, 164–66, 191–92; and war, 146, 175. *See also* antiwar movement; polycentric governance
US military, 15, 19, 23, 40–41, 119, 146, 149, 166, 175, 192. *See also* Vietnam
utopianism, 110–11, 113, 118

Val, Joe, 82–83
van Dresser, Peter, 186
Vietnam, 42–43, 66, 76, 81, 111, 115, 118, 144–45, 150, 158–59, 176, 191
Vigil, Cipriano, 30
Vincent, Craig and Jenny, 23
violence, 9–10, 43, 50–51, 54, 111, 145, 164–65, 175–76
von Briesen, Frances, 89–90, 93–94
von Briesen, Siddiq Hans, 20, *88*, 89–94

war, 9, 15, 54, 79–81, 84, 110, 120, 123, 157, 195. *See also* Vietnam; World War II-era
Washington State, 59–60, 62–63

water issues, 25, 30, 75, 99, 101, 114, 151, 157, 160, 166–67, 172–74, 195
watershed, the, 61–62, 178–79, 196
Watson, Bonnie, 74
Watson, Doc, 82
Wavy Gravy, 23, 70, 72, 76, 118
Wayland, Massachusetts, 79–81, 83–84
Werber, Frank, 65
West Coast, 16, 62–63, 84, 163
West, Jerry, 145–46
Westerman, Floyd Red Crow, 54, 76
Whalen, Philip, 16, 57, *58*, 59–60, 62
Whitman, Walt, 31, 115
Whole Earth Catalog, The, 21, 105, 117, 186
Wilderness Society, 176
Witt-Diamant, Ruth, 59
Woodstock Festival, 21, 23, 72, 73, 118, 123
World War II, 49–51, 57, 79–80, 83, 100, 118–19, 145, 191
writers, 42; activism of, 30–31, 66, 76–77; in California, 35, 66, 187; and counterculture, 57, 81, 187; as environmentalists, 28, 191; Hispano, 120–21; in New Mexico, 76–77, 120–21. *See also* literary movement; poets; specific cities; specific names

yoga, 55, 73–74, 105
Yogi Bhajan, 23, 73, 74, 105
youth movements, 51–53, 79–82, 111, 113, 123